D0709382

COVENANT OVER MIDDLE EASTERN WATERS

Also by Joyce Shira Starr

The Politics of Scarcity:
Water in the Middle East (co-editor)

Kissing Through Glass: The Invisible
Shield Between Americans and Israelis

Faxes to God

Joyce Shira Starr

COVENANT OVER MIDDLE EASTERN WATERS

Key to World Survival

HENRY HOLT AND COMPANY ✦ NEW YORK

Henry Holt and Company, Inc.
Publishers since 1866
115 West 18th Street
New York, New York 10011

Henry Holt® is a registered
trademark of Henry Holt and Company, Inc.

Published in Canada by Fitzhenry & Whiteside Ltd.,
195 Allstate Parkway, Markham, Ontario L3R 4T8.

Library of Congress Cataloging-in-Publication Data
Starr, Joyce.
Covenant over Middle Eastern waters: key to world survival /
by Joyce Shira Starr.
p. cm.
Includes index.
1. Water resources development—Middle East. 2. Water-supply—Middle East. 3. Water-supply—Political aspects—Middle East.
I. Title.
HD1698.M53S72 1995 94-45433
333.91'00956—dc20 CIP
ISBN 0-8050-3019-0

Henry Holt books are available for special promotions and premiums.
For details contact: Director, Special Markets.

First Edition—1995

Designed by Victoria Hartman
Maps by Jeffrey L. Ward

Printed in the United States of America
All first editions are printed on acid-free paper.∞
10 9 8 7 6 5 4 3 2 1

In Loving Memory
of Rafael and Ratzi

ACKNOWLEDGMENTS

My gratitude to agent Karen Gantz Zahler for her dedication in championing this work, and to editor Cynthia Vartan, for so adeptly challenging me toward its realization.

To the four people who sustained this work from its inception with encouragement and counsel; your generosity defines the word *friendship:* writer Frank W. Martin, for sage and stalwart guidance in the artistry of words; Ralph Katrosh, for the shelter of his wisdom; Cassandra Spears, for unwavering insights and special ability to hear; and Maggie Crocker, for her steady confidence in the larger purpose.

I am also indebted to Nadine Cohodas, Chaim Lauer, and Zalman Enav for their penetrating comments on the manuscript, to copyeditor Michael Cain, and to the many who shared their experiences along the way.

And to my family, Rae, Reuben, and Robert Starr—who provided anchor through the cresting waves of this voyage—there can be no friendship deeper or more enduring than yours.

CONTENTS

PREFACE

The Water Kaleidoscope

The world may be divided between those who prefer the grounded feeling of earth under their feet and those who favor instead the buoyant weightlessness of water, finding haven for reflection and renewal in its soothing embrace. I belong to the latter.

This could explain why a single conversation with an Egyptian minister in 1985 so captivated my interest in the stirring force of Middle East waters. With nary a prior hint of change to come, my professional course was abruptly redirected to the stage of Middle East water theater.

Yet, in seeking over the years to understand both players and script, I nearly overlooked the awesome, transcending might of water. The journey behind this book with many chance detours down unchartered waterways of inquiry, helped me to remember.

It became vividly apparent, finally, that true significance

of these waters, and their impact on the world, must be observed through a kaleidoscope that blends the realm of modern politics with the prisms of biblical culture, faith, and spirit from which it took root.

Viewed through the wider lens, Middle East waters can lead us to the essence of life.

I want to know God's thoughts.
All the rest are details.

✦ ✦ ✦

—Albert Einstein

ROMANIA
RUSSIA
Black Sea
BULGARIA
GEORGIA
Istanbul
ARMENIA
Tigris-Euphrates Basin
Ankara
TURKEY
SOUTHEAST
ANATOLIA
Aleppo
ASSYRIA
GREECE
CYPRUS
MESOPOTAMIA
Tigris
SYRIA
Euphrates
Mediterranean Sea
Beirut
Damascus
LEBANON
IRAQ
Baghdad
Jerusalem
Nile Delta
Amman
BABYLONIA
ISRAEL
Alexandria
JORDAN
Cairo
Suez
SINAI
See Map at Right
Nile River
Basin
Nile
Gulf
of Suez
SAUDI ARABIA
EASTERN
DESERT
EGYPT
WESTERN
DESERT
Medina
Aswan
Lake
Nasser
Red Sea
Jidda
Mecca
SUDAN
0 KILOMETERS 500
0 MILES 500

Korazim
GOLAN HEIGHTS
Capernaum
Bethsaida
Tabha
Sea of Galilee
ISRAEL
SYRIA
Zippori
Nazareth
Yarmuk River
Megiddo
Jordan River
JORDAN
Beth-Shean
0 KM 10
0 MILES 10
SAMARIA
WEST BANK
Beirut
LEBANON
Sidon
Damascus
Litani River
Hasbani R.
Mount Hermon
SYRIA
Tyre
GOLAN HEIGHTS
See Inset Above Left
Sea of Galilee (Knerret)
Haifa
Nazareth
Yarmuk R.
Mediterranean Sea
Caesarea
River
SAMARIA
WEST BANK
Tel Aviv
Jordan
Amman
Jericho
Jerusalem
Jordan River Basin
JUDAEA
Gaza
CANAAN
Mamre
Hebron
Dead Sea (Salt Sea)
GAZA STRIP
Beersheba
Sodom and Gomorrah
LOT'S WIFE
ISRAEL
NEGEV
DESERT
JORDAN
SINAI
ARAVA
EGYPT
Eilat
Aqaba
Gulf of Eilat/Aqaba
0 KM 50
0 MILES 50
Jeffrey L. Ward 1995
Tehran
IRAN
Shatt al Arab
Basra
Kuwait City
KUWAIT
Persian Gulf
BAHRAIN
QATAR
Riyadh
UNITED ARAB EMIRATES
YEMEN

INTRODUCTION

Where Once Stood the Tent of Abraham: Past as Prologue

Then the Lord said, "The outrage of Sodom and Gomorrah is so great, and their sin so grave!" . . . As the sun rose upon the earth and Lot entered Zoar, the Lord rained upon Sodom and Gomorrah sulfurous fire from the Lord out of heaven. He annihilated those cities and the entire Plain, and all the inhabitants of the cities and the vegetation of the ground. Lot's wife looked back, and she thereupon turned into a pillar of salt.

—Genesis 20: 23–26

Lot's Wife looks eastward toward Jordan, peering at the future—the end of the Dead Sea. According to legend, the annihilated cities of Sodom and Gomorrah once stood at the southern tip of the Dead Sea valley, the lowest site on earth.

Upon hearing God's plan to rid the earth of the "outrage" of Sodom and Gomorrah, Abraham challenged the

Almighty to save the innocent. The Lord responded by sending two angels to rescue Abraham's nephew, Lot, as well as Lot's two daughters and wife.

This woman of no given name, who recklessly looked back upon the demolition of the flourishing but sinful biblical civilization, presides today over a wasteland of industrial mining that drains the mineral life force from biblical waters.

A lonely rock formation poised at the edge of a tower of stone, Lot's Wife stands statuesque but shriveled. There are no birds, no trees, not even the whisper of the wind in her small enclave of silence. The stony earth over which she holds court is tinged by gray and black, in contrast to the copper-colored majesty of the Dead Sea mountains.

A small earthquake caused the mountain to fracture some years ago, throwing its debris across an ancient caravan road still in service. A new road was quickly constructed only a few feet away, leaving the stones undisturbed in their fallen state.

It was a hot September day of 1993 when I first met Lot's Wife, having traveled three hours from Tel Aviv to see her. Shmaya Ben-David, a colleague with Israel's National Parks Authority, amused by the somewhat eccentric request, had agreed to accompany me to this rendezvous.

Shmaya brought the large van to a sudden stop at the edge of the narrow coastal road. I descended high-spirited with anticipation, while he disembarked more casually—viewing the journey as a pleasant drive, but no more.

Yet suddenly and inexplicably, we were both overtaken by a foreboding sense of loss. "Perhaps we are feeling the sadness of the woman because she is trying to warn us," offered Shmaya unexpectedly. "Just as she once looked back upon the past," he said, "today she stares sorrowfully east at the future."

Had the rocks collapsed from her vain efforts to cry out, to gain our attention? "No one tried to help her," he continued. "Rather than touch the remnants of her pillar, they preferred to build a new road instead."

Fed solely by the River Jordan, the Dead Sea's waters are stolen daily by an unrelenting sun stationed high above, and by mankind acting under the guise of progress. Its level has plummeted by thirty-five feet in the twentieth century, largely due to excessive use of the water of the Jordan River.

The sea, which had two legs for tens of thousands of years, today has only one. The southern end was drained of its waters in 1981 by secret agreement of Jordan and Israel. While the northern seascape is painted in vast swatches of turquoise, the southern area has been turned into a ghostly matrix of ponds used for the mining of salt and other minerals.

Israeli and Jordanian factories based along the sea harvest the salts for use in the production of nearly 10 percent of the world's fertilizers and a third of our pesticides. These towers of technology, looking like pieces of a science-fiction film set, gulp up the bounty, while rusted machinery decorates the parched shoreline.

A 1994 law, passed during Israel's Year of the Environment, allows the Dead Sea Works to further develop the southern waters and adjacent land, all but free of environmental control. These policies are mirrored on the Jordanian side.

Flocks of birds hover over the northern reaches of the sea, where shittah trees line the coast, but the winged creatures instinctively avoid the depleted southern waters. "When you see birds, you see life," said Shmaya.

I stood transfixed, looking upward toward Lot's Wife, then eastward to the exploited sea, and upward again.

Waiting. A car appeared on the horizon, but it was difficult to move. My personal odyssey, a decade's quest over Middle Eastern waters, was to come full circle with this encounter, or so I had been advised by a person especially gifted with spiritual insight.

Expectations were naturally constrained. Serious foreign-policy writers have little latitude to dream or ponder that which cannot be seen or counted. The rational intellect insists that the nonobjective universe is outside the frame of proper analysis.

Still, I was disappointed. The rocky statue that hinted at release from the troubling allure of these ancient waters had only driven me deeper into their plight.

✦ ✦ ✦

It was 4:48 P.M. as we turned back up the road toward Jerusalem. The air was sandy and sweet, replete with Jordanian flies traveling westward to Israel, without flag or diplomatic passport.

Red sandstone mountains on the Israeli coastline suddenly turned to gray and white, then just as quickly to pink, and within seconds to gold. Jordan's Edom mountains, red as their name at sunset, covered the Dead Sea with a scarf of purple that slowly faded into a soft creamy haze.

Subtle changes in both the world above and the world below were reflected in the water. Dazzling purple flowers and silver-green shrubs appeared to be growing upside-down in its muddy reaches.

The sea's salty treasure was carried by the evening breeze as a gift of silky oil to the skin. Salt-kissed air, perhaps the purest on earth, filled my lungs with joy and lightness.

Calmed by the muted palette of colors that speckled the terrain, I thought again of the words of Eren, a former policewoman and a person gifted with insight. A mutual friend had suggested, indeed insisted, that I meet Eren, but with no clear indication as to purpose or gain.

We sat in a busy coffee shop in the heart of Tel Aviv. Eren's face was youthful. Traces of gray laced auburn hair pulled back in a simple ponytail. I took out a notepad, but Eren asked that I rely on memory instead.

The conversation was slow to take root. At my mention of involvement in water issues, however, she began to speak urgently and emotionally of the Dead Sea.

"Think of it this way," she said. "The blood that flows through our veins is the body's water. Blood is salty. Most of the water of the planet is salty. Salt is the purest form of water, and the crystallized Dead Sea is the purest water on earth."

If human history is in the DNA of our blood, so the history of the planet is written in water, Eren continued. The global water system is the blood of the planet, with the purest of information crystallized as salt.

"Water has power, and the Dead Sea is the most powerful of all," she said. "As Lot's Wife can attest, it is here that our connection to life, to the force of light, and to God, is crystallized. The Dead Sea is the repository of crystallized answers to questions we either no longer remember or we fear to ask."

If this were so, I wondered aloud, could Middle Eastern waters be carrying the memory of Abraham, Moses, Jesus, and Muhammad, and the times in which they lived? Might these holy waters also transmit a form of intelligence unfathomable to us through our limited language?

Eren did not respond directly. She stated only that the

journey to find the true meaning of water must be a solitary one.

With night upon us, Shmaya began to increase his speed to overtake the darkness. Remembering Lot's Wife, I found myself regretting the widening distance from the Dead Sea, and from questions not yet fully grasped.

It would take a further year of searching and another visit to the sea before I could fully understand.

FROM THE SPIRITUAL...

DEITIES AND POWERS

Praise him, ye heavens of heavens,
and ye waters that be above the heavens.
—Psalms 148:4

Our common heritage, and our common destiny, is rooted in the parched streams and ebbing rivers of the Middle East. The passions Middle East players bring to the diplomatic water table are informed by the teachings, the power, of the Book. The very source documents of Middle East history—the Old Testament, New Testament, and Koran—serve as clarion guides to an understanding of the cultural meaning of water thousands of years ago, and of its crucial role as we enter a new millennium.

A striking number of significant tales threaded through these treasured sources refer to water, wells, cisterns, streams, rain, seas, and life-sustaining rivers. The Old Testament carries over two hundred water-related passages and verses, and the New Testament over one hundred. More than fifty such verses flow through the Koran.

In time, however, the creeping "secularization" of water subjected this precious resource to mankind's mercy. Over the centuries, water has been used, controlled, manipulated, and treated as humans desire, thus propelling us upon a perilous voyage.

Only by turning once again to the wellsprings of monotheistic inspiration can we recognize—in time—that the fears, "rights," rituals, and laws governing today's conflict over water were actually cast in the biblical era. The quest for control over these sacred waters could support or sunder the ark of our survival.

Oracles and Soothsayers

Men's courses will foreshadow certain ends, as Charles Dickens wrote, but if these courses are departed from, the ends will change.

Why should a flood-weary Midwesterner or Georgian, a rain-logged European, or a snow-fatigued Canadian care about the micropolitics of scarce Middle Eastern waters? Because the earth and its elements, the human spirit and the spirit of the world, are cut from the same vast cloth.

Just as deadly chemicals dumped into the waters of Atlanta, Georgia, reappear in Canada, and life-threatening toxins drained into the Aral Sea are reingested thousands of miles away by newborn babies through their mothers' milk, so too the steaming and swirling hatreds over biblical Middle Eastern waters are a threat far beyond their immediate reality.

The human being, it has been said, is little more than a bag of ancient water on stilts. This magic colorless liquid is essential to human survival. A human fetus is approximately 90 percent water, a newborn 70 percent, and an adult almost 60 percent.

Life is based on water and carbon, explains Gerald Shroeder in *Genesis and the Big Bang,* a highly acclaimed exegesis on parallels between the Book of Genesis and scientific realities. "Without carbon and water," he wrote, "you and I and all the biosphere would not exist." But life as we know it, he emphasizes, "is so special, so complexly organized and so fragile, that it can flourish only within the narrowest environmental conditions."[1]

These narrow conditions take on added urgency when one considers the chorus of voices, both prophetic and scientific, predicting environmental and political upheaval by the turn of the century.

The New Testament, it should be recalled, warns that Armageddon, the ultimate battle against the forces of God, will be fought at Mount Megiddo in Israel. Flashes of lightning, rumblings, peals of thunder, and a violent earthquake "such as had not occurred since people were upon the earth," will emanate from this site (Rev. 16:16–18). The sixteenth-century seer Nostradamus foretells catastrophic floods and drought in the final years of this decade.[2]

Prophesies aside, the world is already in the grip of tumultuous climatic shifts, terrifying earth tremors, plagues, and political instability fraught with the potential for unspeakable human destruction.

In *Beyond the Fall of Night,* science-fiction writers Arthur Clarke and Arthur Banford describe a future century when the planet will be covered by desert, and only Diaspar, a city fortified by walls, amnesia, and fear, will have survived. Reality, however, competes with this fiction of the loss of life-sustaining waters.

Twenty-five nations are already beset by chronic water shortages, with the number expected to rise to ninety in the early twenty-first century. Half of the world population could be mired in drought, famine, or related malnutrition and disease by 2025.

Virtually all of northern Africa, pockets of India, Mexico, China, and the western United States, and almost the entire Middle East region will have entered chronic water shortages during the 1990s. The competition grows fierce. Among the 214 international river and lake basins, 156 are shared by two countries, 36 by three nations, and 22 by up to a dozen countries. Two billion people depend on cooperation with neighboring states for a guaranteed water supply.

The impending water crisis is often compared to the oil shortages of the 1970s, a dramatic but inaccurate parallel. For water is uniquely renewed through the "magic" of the hydrologic cycle that ensures a constant annual supply. Our planetary waters have not increased since the beginning of time.

More than two-thirds of the earth's surface is covered by water. But over 97 percent resides in oceans, inaccessible for human use except at a prohibitive cost. Only 2.59 percent is freshwater, most of it embedded in ice caps and glaciers, buried deep underground, or lost in the atmosphere, leaving an accessible fraction of 1 percent.

Or more starkly: Of all freshwater, only about one-third of 1 percent is available for human survival.

The hydrologic cycle provides forty thousand cubic kilometers of freshwater each year, which could theoretically meet all human needs. Less than a third is usable by human beings, however, and of that, five thousand cubic kilometers flow in uninhabited regions. Hydrologists refer to the remaining water as the gross yield—that fraction of the hydrologic cycle that can reasonably be put to human use.

Although water consumption throughout the world is still less than the limited freshwater supply, to channel freshwater to places where it is vitally needed, at an acceptable price, is an awesome challenge.

What will the future look like if water demand continues to increase? When demand exceeds 50 percent of the gross yield, the potential for water shortages escalates. At the current annual rate of increase, which averaged 4.3 percent over the past thirty years, we reach this danger point at about the turn of the century.

Biblical and prophetic warnings, it appears, converge with scientific realities at the watering hole.

Reverence for Water

The ancient world embodied water as a powerful, fertile, and central deity.

In the Middle East, the Nile is often depicted as the male god Hapi, with two full breasts, giving life to the northern and southern Nile. Persian waters were guarded by the goddess Analinda. The baalim, or gods, of Assyria maintained their celestial thrones on the banks of streams and springs.

Sumerian tales distinguish between Tiamat, the great mother of the salt waters of chaos and creation, and Aspu, the lord who ruled the "sweet waters" under the earth that filled the rivers and streams.

Ea (also known as Enki) was the Mesopotamian god of freshwater and its sources. As the "creator god who formed and engendered life," he also washed away evil and controlled demons.[3]

The presiding god of Eridu, Ea shared direction and rule

of the universe with his father Anu (according to Sumerian theogony, Anu was the firstborn of the primeval sea), his half-brother Enlil (god of storm, wind, and air), and his half-sister, the mother goddess Ninhursag.

In those days, according to the Sumerian *Epic of Gilgamesh* (third millennium B.C.E.), "the world teemed, the people multiplied, the world bellowed like a wild bull." Enlil reported to the gods in council that "the uproar of mankind is intolerable and sleep is no longer possible by reason of the babel."[4]

When the gods concurred with Enlil's fateful decree that all earthly civilization be destroyed, it was Ea who warned the son of Ubara-Tutu about the coming disaster and secretly provided instructions on the building of an impermeable Ark. Ea whispered to him in a dream, "Oh man of Shurrupak . . . tear down your house and build a boat, abandon possessions and look for life."[5]

When Enlil saw the boat, he was "wrath and swelled with anger," and he demanded, "Has any of the mortals escaped? Not one was to have survived the destruction."[6]

The Tree of Life, the Gilgamesh epic informs us, was rooted along the banks of the Euphrates. Joining the Euphrates with the Tigris through an elaborate network of canals, Ea anchored a lasting testament to water—his own Water House—at the edge of the marshlands.

Almost 4,700 years later, his beloved marshlands, their inhabitants, and all of his water achievements would be subject to another cruel decree of destruction. But this time, no one would rush to intervene.

2

DIVINE WATERS

And the spirit of God hovered over the waters.
—Genesis 1:2

The progenitor and steward of all waters is God. Water, we are told in Genesis 1, is the primal cosmic element. In the beginning the universe consisted of water within water.

The "deep" or primeval ocean was divided at creation into upper and lower waters. God said, "Let there be an expanse in the midst of the water, that it may separate water from water" (Gen. 1:6).

Waters flowing above the expanse or firmament are the source of rain, while the waters below form rivers, seas, lakes, and streams. The Hebrew word for water is *mayim,* while the word for sky, *shammaim* ("there is water"), may flow from the very same root.

Waters above manifest trust in God, while waters below signify trust in one another.

God is described in the Old Testament as the "fountain of living waters" and as the "source of living water." He destroys an evil world with the Great Flood; yet, by establishing a covenant with Noah and by providing an ark of safety for Noah and his family, God saves those worthy of being saved for all time.

> For My part, I am about to bring the Flood—waters upon the earth—to destroy all flesh under the sky in which there is breath of life; everything on earth shall perish. But I will establish My covenant with you, and you shall enter the ark, with your sons, your wife, and your sons' wives. (Gen. 17–18)

The pouring of God's spirit and blessing on his chosen people is compared to water: "When as I pour water on thirsty soil and rain upon dry land, so I will pour out My spirit on your offspring, blessing on your posterity" (Isa. 44:3). He will give water in the wilderness and rivers in the desert, "to give drink to My chosen people" (Isa. 43:20).

Divine struggle with waters and victory over chaos are linked in the Bible to God's saving actions on behalf of Israel and its leaders. His love protects them from drowning in a sea of fear or sorrow: "He reached down from on high, He took me; He drew me out of the mighty waters; He saved me from my fierce enemy, from foes too strong for me" (Ps. 18:17).

The biblical escape from Egypt and the journey to the Promised Land is launched when Miriam, sister of Moses, places her baby brother in a wicker basket among the reeds by the bank of the Nile. *Moses* in Hebrew means "drawn from the water." The letters of Miriam's name are also significant: *mar* ("bitter"), *yam* ("sea"), and *raish* (a letter that connotes healing in the Cabala).

Moses, Aaron, and Miriam are the triad of Sinai desert leadership. Legend recalls that manna fell from heaven on the merit of Moses; clouds of glory pointed the way on the merit of Aaron; and a well of water followed the Jewish people through their Sinai wanderings on the merit of Miriam.

The Torah, the body of Jewish law granted to Moses at Mount Sinai, has been compared by rabbinical scholars to an ocean of immeasurable depth. For the word *torah* derives from the root, *yud raish hai,* which means "to teach or direct." The Torah, therefore, is a philosophy of life extending to all of God's creatures.[1]

Biblical water similes, covering the spectrum of human emotions, describe the loss of strength in Job, fear in Joshua, and compassion in Proverbs: "As face answers to face in water, so does one man's heart to another" (Prov. 27:19).

The wicked in Isaiah are "like a tossing sea, which cannot rest, whose waves cast up mire and mud." Amos calls for justice to roll down like the waters of a perennial stream, while salvation in the Psalms of David is equated with a rescue from the waters of death.

Water, the ultimate tribute of hope, is proffered to God to save the Israelites from the wrath of the Philistines. The prophet Samuel commands the people to gather at Mizpah to pour water on the ground before Yahweh, in order to end the cycle of repeated defeats (I Sam. 7:5–6).

The heroes of King David's guard win distinction by procuring water for the king at the risk of their lives (II Sam. 23:16; I Chron. 11: 17–18).

The forsaking of the Lord by defiling the land, and by turning to foreign gods and foreign powers, is similarly depicted in water analogies: "My people have done a twofold wrong: They have forsaken Me, the Fount of living water, and hewed them out cisterns, broken cisterns, which cannot even hold water" (Jer. 2:13).

Jeremiah's admonition, "What is the good of your going

to Assyria to drink the waters of the Euphrates?" takes on special urgency when Jerusalem is besieged by the Assyrians. The king of Assyria threatens that the city will surely fall under the weight of his sword if the people of Jerusalem "rely on the Lord." "Make your peace with me," he tells them, ". . . and drink water from your cisterns" (Isa. 36:15–16).

Waters of Salvation and Wealth

"God's house," the focal point of cosmic salvation for the Jewish people, was founded over the source of the waters of creation.

The Lord told King David: "Your son, whom I will set on your throne in your place shall build the house for My name." And thus, in the 480th year after the Israelites left the land of Egypt, in the 4th year of King Solomon's reign over Israel (approximately 962 B.C.E.), Solomon "began to build the House of the Lord" atop Mount Moriah in Jerusalem.

And when, after seven years, the Temple was completed, Solomon convoked the elders of Israel "to bring the Ark of the Covenant of the Lord from the city of David, that is Zion." God then appeared to Solomon and said, "I consecrate this House which you have built and I set my name there forever. My eyes and heart shall ever be there" (1 Kings 6:1; 8:3).

God himself leads Ezekiel "back to the threshold of the Temple," where the prophet finds water issuing from below its platform. "It was a stream I could not cross." He tells Ezekiel that this miraculous river will transform the Arava region of the Negev Desert into a paradise, and the

Dead Sea, the "sea of stagnant waters," will again become fresh.

Where the river goes, every living creature will survive and even swarms of fish will reappear. Trees will bear fresh fruit every month "because the water from the sanctuary flows to them," while their leaves will be used for healing. Only the swamps and marshes will be left for salt (Ezek. 47:1–13).

King Solomon reminds us that where water is scarce, water is wealth: "I constructed pools of water to irrigate a forest springing up with trees. . . . Thus I gained more wealth than anyone before me in Jerusalem" (Eccles. 2:9).

The Garden of Eden bestowed the gift of four rivers: the Pishon, Gihon, Tigris, and Euphrates. The Tigris joined the Euphrates in nourishing the floodplain that gave rise to Near Eastern civilization.[2] The Euphrates was also the northern boundary of Israelite territory under King David.

Biblical bodies of water conveyed hope, prosperity, and special blessings. The Well of Miriam, the source of life for the Jewish people during their sojourn through the Sinai, is said to rest hidden in Lake Knerret, the Sea of Galilee. Having once located this holy well and experienced the water energy contained within, the fifteenth-century Cabalistic scholar Isaac Luria declared that whoever would immerse himself in the well would never forget the Torah.

The Sea of Galilee may be more than twenty thousand years old. Its southern rim was originally part of an enormous salt lake that once stretched southward almost to Eilat, and that gave birth to the Dead Sea.

Biblical references to the Nile emphasize its impressive flooding, which provided Egypt with water for irrigation and with alluvial soil deposits to renew the fertility of cultivated lands. But dependency on Nile floodwaters could also produce dreaded years of famine. When God turns the Nile into a river of blood, he strikes at the very heart and lifeline of the Egyptian empire (Exod. 4:9; 7:14–22).

Pharaoh's arrogance is underscored by the claim that "my Nile is my own; I made it"; his downfall is initially seeded by his decree that every Hebrew male child will be cast into the Nile. And were it not for the miracle of Moses parting the Red Sea (or, as some scholars suggest, damming a tributary of the Nile), the fleeing Israelites might well have been overwhelmed by the wrathful swords of Egyptian forces, and never have won their historic freedom.

The Jordan, Joshua, and the Ark of the Covenant

The most important biblical conduit, however, is the Jordan River. Running from north of the Sea of Galilee to the Dead Sea, the Jordan River offered the Israelites both strategic and spiritual crossing to the Promised Land. God grants his special blessing to Joshua on the banks of this river.

The Lord informs Joshua, "This day, for the first time, I will exalt you in the sight of all Israel, so that they shall know that I will be with you as I was with Moses. For your part, command the priests who carry the Ark of the Covenant as follows: When you reach the edge of the waters of the Jordan, make a halt in the Jordan" (Josh. 3:7–8).

The Jordan is at flood stage during the harvest months. Yet, when the priests who carry the Ark of the Covenant reach the Jordan River, the upstream waters immediately stop flowing, piling up "at a great distance away, at a town called Adam, . . . while the water flowing down to the

Sea of the Aravah [the Salt Sea] was completely cut off. So the people crossed over opposite Jericho" (Jos. 3:16).

Once the entire Israelite nation has crossed the Jordan, God tells Joshua to select twelve men, one from each tribe, and instruct them to pick up twelve stones "from the spot exactly in the middle of the Jordan, where the priests' feet are standing," and to "deposit them in a place where you will spend the night."

Joshua summons the twelve men whom he has designated, one from each tribe, and instructs them to "walk up to the Ark of the Lord your God, in the middle of the Jordan, and each of you lift a stone onto his shoulder—corresponding to the number of the tribes of Israel. . . .

"This shall serve as a symbol among you," said Joshua. "In time to come, when your children ask, 'What is the meaning of these stones for you,' you shall tell them . . . these stones shall serve the people of Israel as a memorial for all time" (Josh. 4:1–8).

God's Covenant Was in the Rain

The theological significance of water is earlier expressed in Israel's sojourn through the wilderness. When the well that had faithfully followed the Israelites in the Sinai vanishes upon Miriam's death, the lack of water—or spiritual light—leads to murmuring and doubt against Moses. "Why did you bring us from Egypt to kill us and our children and livestock with thirst?" the people complain.

Moses cries out to the Lord, "What shall I do with this people? Before long they will be stoning me!" God responds to their doubt by commanding Moses to strike the rock of Horeb with the very same rod used to turn the Nile into blood and to divide the Red Sea. The site was thereupon named Massah ("trial") and Meribah ("quarrel"), because the people tried the Lord, saying, "Is the Lord present among us or not?" (Exod. 17:3–6).

By contrast to the desert, Canaan would be replete with waters, "for your God is bringing you into a good land, a land of brooks of water, of fountains and springs, flowing forth in valleys and hills" (Deut. 8:7). This "promise" of abundant waters is a formidable vision for people who have wandered in the desert for forty years.

And yet, as the Israelites soon discovered, while Mesopotamia and Egypt were nurtured by bountiful rivers, Canaan was fed primarily by rain. In this "land which the Lord your God looks after," rainfall would be the single most important manifestation of God's power: "But the land you are about to cross into and possess, a land of hills and valleys, soaks up its water from the rains of heaven" (Deut. 11:11–12).

Prayers, fasts, and acts of repentence throughout the Bible beseech God to bestow His blessing of rain in times of drought. The Second Temple–period ritual of the Feast of Water Drawing *(simhat beit hasho'eva),* specifically linked to the fall rains, contains a myriad of rainmaking imagery.

Elijah confronts and overcomes the blasphemous prophets of Baal on Mount Carmel by producing long-awaited rainfall. Conversely, the warning that "I shall shut up the heavens so there will be no rain" is the worst curse of the Bible. God's ability to direct the timing of the rain was no less important than the flow of water itself.

When the Israelites place their faith in a king over God, the prophet Samuel prays for rain as a punishment. For overly abundant waters flowing from heaven on the day of harvest could kill the crop and lead to starvation. But the Israelites refuse to listen to Samuel, stubbornly insisting that only by having a king would they be like other nations. "Let our king rule over us and go out at our head and fight our battles," they declared.

Samuel responds, "It is the season of the wheat harvest. I will pray to the Lord and He will send thunder and rain; then you will take thought and realize what a thing you did in the sight of the Lord when you asked for a king" (Sam. 8:3–12:16).

The story is also told of Rabbi Honi Hame'agel, who drew a circle around himself and declared that he would not move until God provided rain. When a torrential storm followed, the rabbi again cried out to the Lord, but this time beseeched Him to reduce the rainfall to a normal level.

Water's Healing Power

The Cabala, said to be the "soul" of the law given by God to Moses, defines the energy of water as mercy and its purity as sharing. The impurity of water is equated with selfishness. The Hebrew term *maim haim* refers to "living waters," such as springs or rivers. The *mikvah,* a body of living spring- or rainwater, is a channel for positive energies and spiritual balance.[3]

Utilized by women after the period of menstruation, the *mikvah* is also used by men to remove *klippot*—"evil husks" created by man's negative deeds, which "cover" and limit man in his spiritual development. *Klippot* are barriers between man and the light of God.

The ancient *mikvah* derives from the relationship between water and Abraham, father of both Isaac and Ishmael. The Zohar, the basic book of the Cabala, relates that before Abraham would invite a guest into his tent, he would first determine if the visitor's energy was balanced. Spiritual harmony could be restored by bathing in a small spring that ran by his tent in the area of Beersheva.

Rabbi Shimon, who was "chosen" to set down the teachings of the Zohar, was sentenced to death by the Romans for accusing them of intolerance and cruelty. He fled with his son Elazar to a cave in the mountains of Galilee, where they hid for thirteen years until the Emperor's death made it safe to depart. By that time, both the rabbi and his son were covered with sores. Their bodies were miraculously healed when they immersed themselves in hot springs bubbling near the mouth of the cave.

Ezekiel proclaims that true internal cleansing with water will take place in the new age, according to God's promise: "I will sprinkle clean water upon you and you shall be clean from all your uncleanness" (Ezek. 36:25).

The rivers of Damascus were also famous for their healing properties. Thus we can understand the indignation of Naaman, army commander of the king of Aram, upon being instructed by the Israeli prophet Elijah that his leprosy could be cured only by bathing in the River Jordan seven times. "Are not Abana and Pharpar, rivers of Damascus, better than all the waters of Israel?" he demands. "I could bathe in them and be clean!"

Urged on by his servants ("If the prophet told you to do something difficult, would you not do it?"), Naaman immerses himself in the Jordan seven times, "and his flesh became like a little boy's, and he was clean" (2 Kings 5:12–14).

First Covenant in the Promised Land

The first covenant forged in the land of Canaan was over water. When the servants of the Philistine King Abimelech seize a well belonging to Abraham, he reproaches Abimelech with the act. Abimelech feigns ignorance: "I do not know who did this; you did not tell me, nor have I heard of it until today."

Abraham initially enables Abimelech to save face by accepting his declaration. He provides Abimelech with sheep and oxen, "and the two men made a covenant." But Abraham then cleverly sets apart seven lambs of the flock. When Abimelech inquires as to the reason, Abraham explains that by accepting the seven ewes from his hand, Abimelech "became witness for me that I had dug the well." The place was therefore called Beersheva, because the two men swore an oath (Gen. 21:25–31).

The dual relationship between water and a secure presence in the promised land is further highlighted when Isaac's herdsmen begin redigging wells first discovered by Abraham, but closed down by the Philistines after his death. The herdsmen of Gerar quarrel with Isaac's men, saying, "This water belongs to us." Isaac henceforth referred to the first well uncovered as Esek, "because they had quarreled with him."

When the herdsmen of Gerar dispute a second well, Isaac names it Sitnah ("harassment" or "feud"). Later he digs yet another well, and when they do not quarrel over it, Isaac names the well Rehoboth ("width"), declaring: "Now at last the Lord has granted us ample space to increase in the land" (Gen. 26:17–22).

After Sarah's death, Abraham sends his trusted servant to find a wife for Isaac among Abraham's kin in the city of

Nahor. The servant reaches the outskirts of the city, makes his camels sit down by the well of water, and prays to the Lord to grant him success, thereby showing steadfast love to his master, Abraham. "I am standing here by the spring of water," the servant tells God.

The maiden Rebecca, daughter of Abraham's kinsmen, offers to provide water not only to the stranger, but also to his camels—though she is well aware that a hundred gallons of water could be required to quench the thirst of such hardy animals. Her compassionate act confirms God's promise to establish His covenant with Abraham's descendants (Gen. 24:16–27).

Who Will Drink First?

Hospitality in the Bible begins with the provision of water. Indeed, water for the washing of feet is the first offering to a guest. When three angels appear near Abraham's tent by the oaks of Mamre, he declares, "If I find favor with you . . . let a little water be brought, and wash your feet."

The failure to share water with strangers entering a town, or even passing by, could engender serious conflict. When the Israelites were prevented from passing through Edom, Ammon, and Moab because the inhabitants refused, even for money, to share a drink of water, inhabitants of these areas were cursed as a result. Two hundred years later, the memory of this hostile action was the root of a bitter war.

By contrast to the immutable rules of personal hospitality, however, Proverbs suggests a more complex approach for the sharing of water by a town or city. The people are directed to "drink water from your own cistern, running waters from your own well. Your springs will . . . be yours alone" (5:15–18).

The Talmud (a code of law based on the Bible, completed in the fifth century C.E.) states that one who digs a cistern for the public may fill his cup and drink, or fill his jar and bring it home, but he is not allowed to sell the water to people who are walking by. Since it is a public cistern, no one may benefit financially from the sale of water.

When the question was raised in the Talmud as to whether the people of the town or foreigners should come first in being allowed to use a well belonging to the town, the conclusion was that the people of the town come first. The requirements of their thirsting animals also supersede the needs of strangers.

Moreover, if a new spring begins to flow, inhabitants of the city from which it emerges may supply themselves from the spring even though its sources are not in their domain. According to rabbinical commentary, when competing needs are of similar magnitude, the city that controls the water takes precedence. Rabbi Jose, a spiritual leader, even argued that the water requirements of a city in need should always take precedence over the lives of others.

The biblical dictum, "Your brother shall live with you—your life comes first," is called upon in the Talmud to explain why an individual with a bottle in the desert may drink the water himself, rather than share with his fellow traveler.

In other words, water may only be shared with others to the extent that the one who possesses the resource is not seriously harmed. Even if foreigners suffer from a serious lack of water, a city cannot put its inhabitants in physical or economic danger to help meet this need.

As it is written in Maimonides' *The Book of Acquisition*:

"When people have fields along a river they water them in the order [of their proximity to the river]. But if one of them wants to dam up the flow of the river so that his field may be watered first, and then reopen it, and another wants to water his field first, the stronger prevails. The cistern nearest to a water channel is filled first in the interest of peace."

Centuries later, this debate over the "right of thirst" and the right of control over contested water sources dominates the Middle East peace process.

Whoever Shall Defend the Tsinnor

Whoever will touch the *tsinnor* will be a hero, states an obscure biblical sentence relating to David's battle to conquer Jerusalem. *Tsinnor* in modern Hebrew refers to a watershaft or channel. Could *tsinnor* have referred to a water system that David planned to penetrate?

The Jebusites, who controlled Jerusalem, taunted David, saying, "You will never [enter] here. Even the blind and the lame will turn you back." But David told his men, "Those who attack the Jebusites shall reach the water channel *[tsinnor]*" (II Sam. 5:6–8).

Joab, the soldier who succeeded in reaching the *tsinnor,* was appointed commander in chief of David's army. *Tsinnor* is mentioned only one more time in the Bible, in Psalm 42, where the writer's soul "cries for You, O God; . . . in the roar of Your *tsinnor;* all Your breakers and billows have swept over me."[4]

Where life in Mesopotamia or Egypt depended on a system of canals, the earliest Israelite towns and cities were typically established near permanent springs. Beth-Shean, for example, a city located in Galilee and blessed with abundant water, was both a crossroads among nations and a battleground for control over the Holy Land. Twenty layers of civilization have been found beneath its rubble, dating from the fifth millennium B.C.E. to the Roman-Byzantine period. Rising from the dust of history are vast public structures, temples, a seven-thousand-seat Roman theater, elegant colonnaded streets, shops, and even baths with their own special heating system.

The Philistine rulers of Beth-Shean displayed the bodies of Saul and his sons upon its walls, after they were killed in the Battle of Mount Gilboa. But King David succeeded in conquering the city.

To defend against invaders, however, most of the strategic cities of the kingdoms of Judah and Israel were built on hilltops; their sources of water remained outside city walls, down the sloping terrain. With successive rebuildings, the cities were moved progressively farther from their water supplies.

In times of war, this distance could prove fatal, as a city could be deprived of water during long sieges. With little or no rainfall between March and October, cisterns and other rain collectors inside the walls could remain empty for half a year or longer.

Engineering Breakthrough: The Aqueduct

The development of plaster-lined cisterns permitted settlement where springs were lacking or inadequate. But the only portable containers available at the time were made of expensive metal or breakable pottery. We can picture a woman descending the slopes with a clay jar on her head to fetch water from the spring below.

The challenge of ensuring a steady supply of water from

a distant source was finally solved through the engineering breakthrough of aqueducts. King Sennacherib of Assyria, who established the city of Nineveh in the eighth century B.C.E., built the earliest aqueduct yet discovered. This conveyor brought water a distance of thirty miles, irrigating parks and gardens along the way. Razing Babylon in 695 B.C.E., Sennacherib diverted a principal irrigation canal so that its waters would cover the ruins.

When Sennacherib invaded Judah and encamped against its fortified towns, King Hezekiah of Jerusalem consulted with his officers and warriors about stopping the flow of the springs outside the city walls. The Bible reports that Hezekiah acted with vigor, "rebuilding the whole breached wall, raising towers on it, and building another wall outside it" (2 Chron. 32:2).

Fortunately for Hezekiah, the Lord sent an angel to annihilate every mighty warrior, commander, and officer in the army of the king of Assyria, and the precious water was spared. Sennacherib returned in disgrace to his land, where he was slain by his own offspring.

Elaborate tunnels and conduits were also constructed in Hazor, Lachish, Massada, Zippori, and Megiddo to ensure access to streams located at the foot of city walls. Megiddo controlled one of the most important military and trade routes of antiquity, the Via Maris, linking Egypt in the south with Syria, Anatolia, and Mesopotamia to the north and east. Its archaeological treasures even include a broken cuneiform tablet bearing a portion of the Mesopotamian *Epic of Gilgamesh.*[5]

Megiddo was a chariot city under Kings Solomon and Ahab, and home to Solomon's stables; its finely crafted stones lead us to an immense water channel. The city's water problems were solved toward the end of King Ahab's reign, when engineers succeeded in carving a tunnel through stone and earth to reach a spring at the foot of the mound. A huge vertical shaft was first dug inside the city, followed by the construction of a horizontal tunnel.[6]

When completed, the tunnel stood, rather amazingly, at exactly the same height as the spring, so that the springwater could flow through it to the city. The entrance to the cave containing the spring was camouflaged with rocks and soil.

Cities located in the southern areas of Israel, by contrast, faced (then and now) quite a different problem from Megiddo, for the southern desert areas cannot absorb plentiful water. Rainfall, scarce during most of the year, brings massive floods during winter. Some researchers believe that the true purpose of Jericho's wall, built during the eighth and seventh millennia B.C.E., was to stop these flood currents and to prevent the settlement from being inundated.

King Herod, builder of the mountain fortification of Massada near the Dead Sea, harnessed desert flood waters by constructing a dam across the valley. The dam directed the water by aqueduct to a system of cisterns ingeniously cut into the slope of the mountain, and from there to a protected path snaking upward to the summit of Massada, and a further maze of cisterns.

When the lower cisterns were filled to capacity by winter rains, excess water was carried by donkeys to the cisterns above, which were covered with a waterproof layer of plaster. King Herod's Massada, a waterless rock, also featured expansive baths and even swimming pools![7] Archaeologists are still unable to explain how such technical solutions and feats of engineering were achieved during biblical times.

Ingenuity in diverting river waters was also evidenced by

Egyptian, Median (Persian), and Babylonian forces in their successful attack on Nineveh, the capital of Assyria, when they created a flood plain for elevating their siege engines onto rafts.

The rivers of Babylon, where Jewish exiles lamented the loss of Zion, were also used by Nebuchadnezzar as a moat to defend his inner castle.[8]

The Voyage of Jesus

Water's centrality to the teachings of Jesus reflected the cultural period in which he lived. Baptism (immersion in living water) signified purification, regeneration, and entry into God's kingdom. It was during Jesus' own baptism in the Jordan River, performed by his cousin John the Baptist, that "the heavens were opened unto him, and he saw the Spirit of God descending like a dove" (Matt. 3:16).

When a woman of Samaria comes to draw water from Jacob's well, near the plot of ground that Jacob had given to his son Joseph, Jesus requests a drink of this "living" water. She is shocked by the request, since Jews of that period were prohibited from dealings with Samaritans.

To the question posed by Nicodemus, "How can a man be born when he is old?" Jesus replied, "Except a man be born of water and the Spirit, he cannot enter into the kingdom of God." Those "born of water" were also compared by his disciples to God's chosen who survived the Flood (John 3:5; 1 Pet. 3:20).

Jesus' decision to wash the feet of his followers, even as he was preparing for his own death, conveyed the ultimate message of humility: "Verily, verily, I say unto you, The servant is not greater than his lord" (John 13:16).

From the sloping hilltop hamlet of Nazareth, Jesus surely watched the soft morning sun climb slowly over Zippori, the largest Jewish city in the lower Galilee valley. Zippori is renowned for its magnificent Nile Mosaic celebrating God's gracious water blessings with a feast of images wedding water, animals, and mankind.

Jesus would have walked to Zippori along the course of the life-giving water, which flowed from the sloping hills of sleepy Nazareth to the bustling city below, or perhaps through the Nazareth-Zippori aqueduct buried deep beneath the earth, a remarkable tunnel of crimson-colored caverns.

His spiritual voyage, however, took him from shore to shore of the sapphire Sea of Galilee. It was at the water's edge of the town of Tabha that Jesus performed the Miracle of the Loaves and Fishes, and from the shore at Tabha that Jesus walked on water.

After the miraculous feeding, Jesus bade his disciples "to get back into the boat and go before him to the other side, to Bethsaida," while he dismissed the crowd. He then climbed the mountain to pray, remaining alone until evening, when he could see that his disciples "were making headway painfully," given the strong wind against them. At the fourth watch of the night Jesus came to them, "walking on the sea."

> He meant to pass by them, but when they saw him walking on the sea they thought it was a ghost, and cried out; for they all saw him and were terrified. But immediately he spoke to them and said, "Take heart, it is I; have no fear." And he got into

> the boat with them and the wind ceased." (Mark 6:45–51)

A second storm appears in the Gospels when Jesus sails with his disciples from Capernaum to Kursi. As they sailed, he fell asleep. Even as a great tempest arose, swamping the ship with waves, Jesus remained in slumber. When his disciples awoke him saying, "Save us. We are perishing," Jesus asked, "Why are you afraid, you of so little faith?" He then arose, "rebuked the winds and the sea, and there was a dead calm" (Matt. 8:23–26).

Kursi, a center of idol worship, was a fishing village in the northwestern corner of the Hippene, a pagan area where Satan purportedly reigned supreme. As Jesus climbed out of his boat, a man possessed by demons cried out, "Leave me alone! Have you come here to torture me?"

Jesus instructed the demons to depart from the man, allowing the unclean spirits to enter a herd of pigs feeding on a nearby hillside. The herd, numbering about two thousand, suddenly "rushed down the steep bank into the sea, and were drowned in the sea" (Mark 5:13).

Jesus also preached in Korazim, an ancient Jewish city famous for its grain, and it was here that he decried a lack of faith in his message ("Woe to you, Korazim"). A majestic black basalt synagogue, decorated with carvings of flora and fauna, and with a black basalt chair inscribed as the seat of Moses, rests at the center and highest point of this city upon a hill. A *mikvah* was also unearthed here, along with an olive press, granary, and cistern, poignant remnants of pulsating life in biblical times.

While Jesus performed miracles in Tabha, Korazim, Kursi, and Bethsaida, however, he always began his travels from Capernaum, a city by the Sea of Galilee. And to Capernaum he would faithfully return: "Jesus stepped into a boat, crossed over and came to his own town" (Matt. 9:1).

Indeed, it was "by the sea" or "in a boat" that Jesus often preferred to share his thoughts with the people of Galilee, conveying in his teachings the spiritual gift of water that derived from Jewish roots.

Sukkot, or the Feast of Tabernacles, celebrating the end of one agricultural year and the beginning of the next, also brings ardent prayers for rain. On the last and great day of the feast, Hoshana Rabba, when rituals representing the plea for rain reached their culmination, Jesus cried out to the people assembled in Jerusalem, "Let anyone who is thirsty come to me, and let him who believes in me drink" (John 7:37). His choice of imagery spoke directly to the longing for bountiful, living waters.

3

ISHMAEL AND THE WELL OF WATER

For a Muslim, Judaism, like Christianity, is a
superseded predecessor of Islam. The Jewish and
Christian scriptures were authentic divine
revelations . . . replaced by God's
final and perfect revelation.

—Bernard Lewis,
The Jews of Islam, 1984

Muhammad taught that portions of the Old and New Testaments were divinely inspired, but that the Koran was revealed to him as the final word of God.

Intimately connected with the Judaic tradition through their common ancestor, Abraham, and through the concept of one god, Islam and Judaism bear close resemblance. Abraham is referred to in the Koran as the first Muslim and "the Friend of God."[1]

Abraham's firstborn, Ishmael, was conceived by Hagar, a slavewoman. When Sarah demanded that both mother and son depart, Abraham prepared a skin of water before sending Hagar into the wilderness of Beersheva.

Once the water was gone, Hagar cast the child under a

bush. Weeping, she sat at a far distance so as not to witness his death. But God opened her eyes to see a well of water, thus assuring the continuity of Ishmael's seed (Gen. 21:18). The well, known as Zum Zum in Arabic, is said to be located at Mecca.

The Koran: Holy Waters

The Koran, the holy scripture of Islam, describes water as the very source of creation. "We made from water every living thing. Will they not then believe?" (Sura XXI).

Admittance to "gardens with rivers flowing beneath" is the promise of life to come, a theme reiterated throughout the Koran: "Those who obey God and His Apostle will be admitted to Gardens with rivers flowing beneath, to abide therein [forever] and that will be the Supreme achievement" (Sura IV).

The punishment for transgression, however, is boiling and scalding waters. God will say, "Such is [the end of] those who deliver themselves to ruin by their own acts: they will have for drink [only] boiling water," and God will pour over the head of the sinner "the Penalty of Boiling water" (Sura V; XLIV).

The name of the Shari'a, the whole of Islamic law comprising the Koran, the sunna, *imja'* (consensus), and *qiyas* (analogy), literally means: "The path to the watering place."

The Muslim claim to Jerusalem, it should be noted, derives from Muhammad's early revelation that holy city should be the path of prayer, and later from his nocturnal journey to the city, from where it is said that he ascended to heaven.

Upon capturing Jerusalem in 637 C.E., the caliph Omar refused to pray at the Church of the Holy Sepulchre, fearing that this act would sanction its being transformed into a mosque, a sign of disrespect. Asking to be taken instead to Mount Moriah, he was brought to a large rock covered with debris, and there he prayed.

This Holy Rock, or al-Sakhra, became central to the Islamic faith. Caliph Abd al-Malik created a magnificent oratory over the rock, renowned as Qubbat al-Sakhra, or the Dome of the Rock.[2]

Muslims believe that al-Sakhra is closer to heaven than any other spot on earth and—as the Jews believed of the Temple of Solomon—that all sweet waters originate beneath its divine splendor. They also believe that Noah's Ark rested on the rock after the flood had subsided.

Islamic Water Law

The Koran, a guide for governance no less than for religious practice, is a bridge between the historic and modern management of water by Islamic countries.

Islamic legal principles concerning water are based on the teachings and practices of the Prophet, his companions, their immediate successors, and the imams or religious officials. Water laws reflect the conditions and needs of Arabia at the time of the Prophet, and of other regions penetrated or conquered by Muslims.[3]

Water rights were generally under the purview of the imam, who issued fatwas (decrees) concerning local water disputes. These tended to be frequent in occurrence, given the harsh desert environment.

The imam, in turn, typically relied on government officials, the local treasury, and "volunteers" for execution of the fatwas. Owners of canals, for example, could be forced to undertake annual repairs, on the premise that a failure to do so would diminish the supply of water for those who had a right to it.

In place of a unified body of water law, a blend of unrelated and sometimes conflicting decisions evolved over time. General principles are usually accepted by both Sunni and Shia Muslims, with differences in detail between them.

The right to use water for drinking purposes is expounded in the Shari'a under the right of thirst. Seven sources of water are lawful to use for drinking or ablution: rain, snow, hail, springs, wells, rivers, and the sea. Water from great rivers like the Tigris and Euphrates can be used by all and to any extent for both drinking and irrigation.

Water use from lesser rivers must be based on inquiry into the consequences. Where damming or allocation is necessary to provide enough water for irrigation, the river is normally regarded as the joint property of the riparian cultivators. The question of how much water may be retained by the country closest to the headwaters depends on differing circumstances, such as the season of the year, the type of crop irrigated, etc.

In wells dug for the public benefit, water is freely available to all; the digger has the right of first comer. Tribesmen or individuals who dig wells for their own use have first right to the water as long as they remain in the vicinity, but must share water with persons suffering from thirst. Private ownership of wells cannot be claimed until water has actually been found and the well has been lined.

Natural springs are treated as analogous to permanently flowing rivers. Where the water supply is limited, the first person undertaking an irrigation project has priority; otherwise the water must be shared equally.

Springs discovered by digging become the property of the owner and of the surrounding harem or community. Only persons suffering from thirst have a claim against the owner. If the owner has a surplus of water, he may be obliged to provide it gratis for another man's cattle, but not for irrigating crops.

A person who possesses water in a vessel is its sole owner, and he is not obliged to give it to others free of charge; it is, however, his duty to relieve someone suffering from thirst, in return for compensation.

According to the tradition of the Prophet, desert waters constitute the main object of real property. Groundwater is considered to be a public good, and cannot be individually appropriated. Use is subject to a strict order of priority, with the watering of desert livestock high on the list. No owner of a well can abuse the water.

The Ottoman Empire followed the detailed provisions of the Islamic law, with the basic notion that water, like wild vegetation and fire, was open to use by the public at large; this included seas, large-size lakes, great rivers, and subterranean waters.

The state was generally responsible for large-scale waterworks on the great rivers. Everyone was free to make use of these sources, at no cost, so long as no harm was entailed. Private ownership of water was also recognized. The Muslim concept of water forbade water taxation.

Rulers of Egypt, Persia, Turkey, and the Arab Middle East ensured the continuity of their regimes by protecting their waters. In ancient Egypt, the annual digging and cleaning of irrigation canals was one of the most crucial functions of the sultans under the Ayyubids and the Mamluks. The breakdown in the control of water in Persia was inevitably followed by a decline in prosperity.

Water, like perfume, was employed in Islamic rituals over the making of pacts and alliances. However, since there is no record in Islamic history of international water disputes prior to this century, Muslim law has scant provision concerning cross-boundary conflicts.

Non-Muslim countries are regarded as the abode of war (*dar-al-*harb). Yet, where water rights are concerned, Islamic law speaks of man, and not of Muslims. The seeming contradiction prevails until this very day.

From the Spiritual: In Summary

The current Middle East water crisis is typically portrayed as the result of forces of nature run amok, of poor luck in resource allocations handed down by the fates, or of the whims of anonymous governmental bureaucracies. The illuminating lessons of the Book are but dimly recalled. Mesmerized by the promise of rapid technological solutions, today's leaders fail to comprehend that lasting water security derives from personal responsibility. As a consequence, individual policy-makers and the decisions they take are neatly divorced from the drama. In Jordan, for example, chemical seepage from a poorly constructed treatment facility led in 1990 to the ruination of hundreds of farms. "The politician who chose this system is a criminal," declared the minister of water. "I told the king that this man should be tried in the courts for sabotage and treason."

Upon entry to the afterlife, ancient Egyptians were asked whether they had polluted the Nile or cut down a fruitful tree. The response determined whether a person was received as a good spirit or as a bad spirit. "If this was in the consciousness of ancient Egyptians," asked Bahaddin Bakri, the leader of Egypt's Green Party, "what is the consciousness of modern Egyptians?"[4]

Indeed, what is the water consciousness of Middle Eastern leaders as they preside over the fate of the region? How do they perceive the "value" of water? Are their proposals for its management equal in ingenuity and depth of understanding to those of bygone eras?

II

TO THE REALM OF POWER...

4

WATER POKER:
Playing for Our Lives

The amount of water in the Nile is no more than
when Moses was found in the bulrushes.

—Vice President Al Gore,
Earth in the Balance, 1992

When I entered his office on February 4, 1985, Boutros Boutros-Ghali was nearly sixty, but had the appearance of a man in his late forties. Lean and taut, he was wearing, as always, a perfectly tapered French-cut suit.

The Egyptian's eloquent English resonated with a heavy French accent that could easily wrap his listener in a poetic mist. Well aware of this talent, he had honed it to perfection.

Boutros-Ghali, even then, was a serious man who tended to guard the most basic of emotions. He was a Coptic Christian in a Muslim country. Both his grandfather and his uncle had served as foreign ministers of Egypt, but that was in a different epoch, and Boutros-Ghali was now denied the rank. As minister of state for foreign affairs, he was fated to remain one step below the status of minister.

I had interviewed Boutros-Ghali on prior occasions regarding prospects for the Middle East peace process. Considered the don of regional experts, he was held in awe by journalists and academics alike. Boutros-Ghali was one of the few who had stood by Anwar Sadat in his historic quest for peace with Israel. When his direct superior, the minister for foreign affairs, resigned, it had been Boutros-Ghali who accompanied Sadat to Jerusalem as acting foreign minister.

The man was a tenured professor of international law, Fulbright scholar at Columbia University, author of more than a hundred publications, and was decorated by twenty-five countries for his diplomatic initiatives. A return visit to his high-ceilinged office with its deep red furniture was an intellectual event not to be missed.

I also looked forward to the hour of the appointment: six P.M. The sun would turn meek by then, losing its aggressive hold on the city, while the streets of Cairo would hum rather than shout with angry horns.

The scent of sand and jasmine guided me to a closely guarded, tree-covered gate to power. I mused that the Ministry of Foreign Affairs, a palatial feat of architecture with long empty halls and unfathomable secrets to tell, had, like Brigadoon, reappeared on the horizon precisely at that moment, in honor of my visit. The play would soon begin.

"Water," Boutros-Ghali stated, upon ushering me to a straight backed chair. I thought he was offering a glass of liquid refreshment instead of the usual sugary tea. But before I could open my notebook to a hastily scratched list of questions, he launched into the topic he intended to address. The professor had taken center stage and was not to be distracted from his objective.

"The next war in our region will be over water, not politics," he said. "Washington doesn't take this seriously, because everything for the United States relates to oil."

Egypt's preoccupation in 1985 with a three-year drought —the worst since 1913—was little known in the Western world, he explained, and rarely mentioned in the press. But in Egypt all other issues, including relations with Israel and the peace process, paled by comparison to growing anxieties over water.

A continuation of the African drought into a fourth or fifth year, according to Boutros-Ghali, would have drastically affected Egypt's tourism revenues, since it would make the Nile unnavigable for leisure vessels, and create acute water shortages in hotels. Oil exports would cease, as oil would become the only ready alternative for generating electricity (targeted completion of Egypt's nuclear power facility was almost a decade away). A prolonged drought would mean millions of starving Egyptians.

"Our problem cannot be solved according to classical formulas," Boutros-Ghali insisted. "Without political imagination, Egypt will become a new Bangladesh fraught with drought and famine—but with one difference. This Bangladesh will be on the beaches of the Mediterranean—only one-half hour by jet from the rich people of the north."

"The government is aware of the problem and trying to find a correct approach," stated Boutros-Ghali. "The dilemma is that our people, including most of the elite, do not yet seem to grasp the magnitude of the issue or the potential catastrophe involved."

For over a decade, Boutros-Ghali carried the Egyptian portfolio in negotiations among the nine riparian nations of the Nile Basin. He forged a reputation both for political tenacity and skillful handling of complex resource data.

Upon his appointment as secretary general of the United Nations in January 1992, Boutros-Ghali begged President Hosni Mubarak to appoint the right person to carry on his efforts. The president told him, "Don't worry Boutros, I will personally take responsibility for your work."[1]

"But a president cannot take the time to care about these things," Boutros-Ghali contended. "Therefore all the work I did on the Nile will soon be lost and there is absolutely nothing I can do about it." Asked how he could watch all of his hard work slip away at this historic juncture, he sighed, "I do not have a copyright on warnings over water."

The Perilous Middle East: War Drums Along the Nile

As early as the mid-1980s, U.S. government intelligence services estimated that there were at least ten places in the world where war could break out over dwindling shared water resources—the majority in the Middle East.

Jordan, Israel, the West Bank and Gaza, Cyprus, Malta, and the countries of the Arabian Peninsula are sliding into the perilous zone where all available fresh surface and groundwater supplies will be fully utilized. Morocco, Algeria, Tunisia, and Egypt face similar prospects in ten to twenty years.

Morocco's achievements in the water and sanitation sectors are unparalleled in Africa. Still, the country confronts the prospect of a declining water supply beyond the year 2000, when its current population of 24 million is projected to reach 31 million.

Israel, the West Bank and Gaza, Jordan, the Republic of

Yemen, and Saudi Arabia in the Middle East, and Algeria and Tunisia in North Africa, have already arrived at the threshold of a red-line "water barrier"—the point beyond which vastly accelerated efforts are required to keep pace with spiraling populations.

Approximately 250 million people inhabited the planet two thousand years ago. The number had risen to 1.7 billion by 1900, and to 5.4 billion by 1994. The optimists declare that the limits of population growth will be reached at 8 billion; the pessimists talk of 14 billion people by the middle of the next century.

Middle Eastern and North African countries combined will experience a growth in population of more than 400 million people by the close of the 1990s, pitting the Davidian capacity of existing water and sanitation services against the Goliath of demand. The human toll translates into tragic statistics. UNICEF reports, for example, that thirty-five thousand children worldwide are dying daily from hunger or disease caused by lack of, or contamination of, water. A major percentage of these deaths occur on the African continent.

By the turn of the century, almost 40 percent of the African population will be at risk of death or disease from water scarcity or contamination. Egypt, the Arab pillar of the Mideast peace process, will hardly be immune from the frenzied refugee flows throughout the continent.

"The only matter that could take Egypt to war again is water," declared President Anwar Sadat in the spring of 1979, only days after signing the historic peace treaty with Israel. His unveiled threat was not directed at Israel but at Ethiopia, the upstream nation that controls 85 percent of the headwaters of Egypt's lifeline, the Blue Nile.

"The national security of Egypt is a question of water,"

Boutros-Ghali emphasized in our earlier meeting. When a proposal was floated to transport Nile waters to the Gaza Strip, he was also heard to comment, "Over my dead body."

The Nile is Africa's bridge, linking the northern and southern parts of the continent. This slowly meandering river, one of the longest on earth, forged the fate of Egypt and Africa five thousand years ago, blending civilizations, personalities, and ethnic groups.

"Hence, Egypt became Africa and shall remain Africa, proud of its African authenticity," Egyptian President Hosni Mubarak told participants of the 1990 African Water Summit, which was convened by this writer in cooperation with the Egyptian government. Over forty countries attended.

The Nile provides 86 percent of the 158 billion gallons of water used by Egypt each year. Yet, as the last nation along the river's path, Egypt has scant control over the policies and actions of eight upstream governments.

When the 1982 drought began, the country's critical Aswan reservoir was full. By the beginning of 1985, Egypt had withdrawn more than 50 billion cubic meters of water; it had taken 20 billion in the previous year alone, when the inflow from the Nile was the lowest in fifteen years.

If the drought had continued for another year (which fortunately it did not), the reservoir would have dropped sufficiently to affect power generation. If it had gone on for two more years, Egypt would have used up all of its usable storage. By the third year, the country would have had no power generation, and only enough water to serve two-thirds of the area then being irrigated.

Thereafter, even if the dry spell had ended, the Nile could no longer have supported both Egypt's burgeoning population, expected to reach over 75 million by the turn of the century, and that of the other African nations that look to the Nile for survival.

Egypt supplies its population with free Nile flood water for farming. Any Egyptian, wealthy farmer or peasant, can draw as much water as he pleases from a national canal system below ground level, so long as he can pay the meager price of a pump to bring up the water. "Even my garden is flood-irrigated," a U.S. official confided.

An official attending the African Water Summit organized by this writer in Cairo in June 1990, suggested that, in addition to high-level diplomatic conferences on water, "You should hold a water summit for the farmers along the Nile, so they begin to understand the limits of our resources."

In September 1989, Dr. Boutros-Ghali sounded the water alarm to members of the U.S. Congress. His dismal projection of Egypt's water future bears repeating. If present circumstances continue, he said, Egypt and the Sudan will experience a severe deficit in water resources by the year 2010, of 10 billion cubic meters per year. Both countries receive only about three inches of annual rainfall. The other riparian countries will require a total of at least 10 billion cubic meters per year within twenty years.

"What is worse is that each Nile country expects different benefits from the control and management of water resources," Boutros-Ghali stated. "The other African countries, which have not reached the level of agriculture through irrigation achieved by Egypt, are not as interested in the problem of water scarcity. It is the classic difference in attitudes found among upstream and downstream countries."

Even in the best of circumstances, most of the Nile countries will be unable to generate sufficient capital to finance critically needed water storage and management projects without massive assistance from donor nations and lending institutions. The foreign debt of Africa is already approximately $240 billion, with Nile Basin countries sharing at least $80 billion of that burden.

"We know it will be impossible to get assistance from international organizations and donor countries unless we have not only stability, but also a consensus among us, and we are trying our best to achieve these goals," Boutros-Ghali emphasized.

By invading Kuwait, Iraq forged a link between Egypt's water-security concerns as an African nation and its Middle East national security agenda. The Kuwaiti Fund and Persian Gulf financial institutions announced in July 1991 a commitment to underwrite Egypt's northern Sinai agriculture project, designed by the United Nations, at an estimated cost of $1.3 billion. The end of Kuwaiti sovereignty would mean the loss of this urgently needed funding.

Egypt is desperately searching for means to expand human settlement in the Sinai, to lessen the staggering population burden of Cairo, Alexandria, and other smaller but burgeoning cities. Ninety-seven percent of Egyptian territory is barren desert, and 58 million Egyptians are concentrated in 3 percent of the land. Egypt gains an additional one million in population every ten months. The feared loss of Kuwaiti and Persian Gulf assistance for the expansion of lands for both people and sources of food was an important factor that helped to rally Egypt to the American side in the crisis.

By the year 2000, the Egyptian El Salam or "Peace" Canal will begin carrying more than 3 billion cubic meters of Nile waters under the Suez Canal and along the Mediterranean coast to over one hundred new agricultural villages in the northern Sinai project near El Arish, adding four hundred thousand acres to cultivation. Egypt is offering livestock, money, and "virtually free water" to thousands of young people motivated to farm the desert.[2]

Yet against this backdrop of historic accomplishment, the chairman of Egypt's Water Research Center, Mahmoud Abu-Zeid, readily admitted that "beyond 2000 our water budget is very dark and very serious." Five acres of irrigated desert, moreover, grow only as much as half an acre of Nile river bottomland.[3]

In 1991, more than a decade after Sadat's declaration over water, Egypt's minister of defense, Lieutenant General Mohammed Hussein Tantawi, reiterated Egypt's readiness to use force, if necessary, to protect its control of the Nile River.

"We have forgotten that the Nile is the lifeline of Egypt," he stated in a 1991 interview. "So we are not ruling out the possibility of using some acts of deterrence after exhausting peaceful means in case any party tries to control the river's waters."[4]

Water War Rooms

Water and food security will soon rank with military security in the war rooms of Middle Eastern defense ministries. Strategic coordination of Saudi Arabia's water supplies, for example, is crucial for a kingdom so desperate for water that it relies on fossil aquifers (nonrenewable underground reservoirs) for over 75 percent of its water requirements.

In its major drive for food self-sufficiency, Saudi Arabia joined the ranks of the world's top wheat exporters in

1984. By heavily subsidizing irrigation waters, the Saudis have been producing wheat crops, but at four times the world price.[5]

Sixty percent of the world's desalination capacity is in the Persian Gulf. Saudi Arabia's desalinated water alone exceeds 30 percent of the global production, while Kuwait and all of the other gulf states are almost totally dependent on desalting plants for their freshwater supply and for petrochemical production.

Water, communication, and transportation are fundamental to economic survival, and energy is the common denominator. Leon Awerbuch, manager for power and desalination with Bechtel, has pointed out that almost all of the desalting plants in Saudi Arabia and Kuwait are dual-purpose power facilities.

The Saudis secretly worry that their immense desalination plants, the size of small cities, will become targets for aggression. Indeed, all Persian Gulf states are strategically vulnerable to any power that succeeds in attacking or disrupting their desalting capability.

"It was like a heartbeat when they were all going, and now it has stopped," a technician of Kuwait's Shuwaikh power and desalination station told *National Geographic*'s Priit Vasiland, after Kuwait's oldest station was destroyed by Iraqi soldiers.[6]

Saddam Hussein's missile target practice against Kuwait's refineries produced a "black cloud from hell" over Kuwait waters and land. Blazing oilfields created an impenetrable wall of solid black, and 727 burning wells were churning out rivers of oil. "You would look out of your vehicle and say, 'Jesus Christ, that can't be man-made. It must be the end of the world,' " an American soldier told this writer. Short of war or terrorist actions, however, even the accidental explosion of an oil tanker could critically endanger Persian Gulf desalination plants.

Saudi Arabia's concerns over water became a priority for the U.S. government when it faced the challenge of maintaining several hundred thousand thirsty American troops in the Saudi desert. The price the United States paid to ship water to its troops was at least ten times the price of oil.

Theoretically, the Water Resources Management Action Group (WARMAG), an interagency group under the direction of the Department of Defense, plans for the provision of potable water to troops in the field. In practice, the Defense Department relied on bottled-water plants in Saudi Arabia and the United Arab Emirates for its desert warriors, and bottled water from Turkey for troops that entered Kuwait.

The United States shipped portable desalination units to Saudi Arabia, as well as massive ice-makers that would supplement an overstressed factory in Bahrain. On military aircraft, water tankers were given as high a priority as armor or weaponry. A special reserve unit dealing with water supply was activated, and American experts were assigned to identify water sources in unpopulated areas close to the Kuwaiti and Iraqi borders.

In spite of these experiences, the Iraqi crisis did not lead to an integrated water plan for regional strategic defense. According to Edward Badolato, former deputy assistant secretary for energy emergencies at the U.S. Department of Energy, the U.S. government "is doing nothing" to anticipate sabotage of pumping stations, treatment plants, pipelines, or dams in the Middle East.

Over a thousand terrorist attacks were directed against energy targets around the world last year. The U.S. Army Corps of Engineers, which built a four-thousand-airman camp in Saudi Arabia with state-of-the-art engineering, has developed defensive security plans relative to domestic facilities, but not internationally. "We're not equipped to deal with it," Badolato emphasized. "We haven't focused on the water problem. We're barely capable of focusing on oil."[7]

The more important waterworks in Saudi Arabia, as in other Middle Eastern countries, are loosely ringed by troops and checkpoints —and even equipped with a few missiles—but the overall level of protection, insisted Badolato, is no greater than that provided to postal or telephone systems.

5

SEARCHING FOR THE HOLY GRAIN

> Nahmanides taught that at the beginning, all
> that is on and within the Earth and all the heavens,
> in fact all the universe, was somehow packed,
> compressed, squeezed into this speck of space,
> the size of a mustard grain.
>
> —Gerald L. Schroeder,
> *Genesis and the Big Bang*

In days to come Jacob shall strike root, Israel shall sprout and blossom, and the face of the world shall be covered with fruit," spoke the prophet Isaiah (27:6).

The "ultimate obscenity," predicted George Orwell nearly three thousand years later, "will be when half the world watches the other half starve."

Food insecurity stalks the global horizon like a ghostly villain in a postmidnight television movie. Short of casting Harrison Ford as the hero, however, few people are gripped by a plot that centers upon seeds and water—or the lack thereof.

"If present trends continue, we will not be able to feed the world's population," concluded Paul Kennedy, author of *The Rise and Fall of the Great Powers* and *Preparing for the Twenty-first Century,* at the 1992 Davos World Economic Forum.

"If we reach the point where half the world watches the other half starve," cautioned Lester Brown, president of the Worldwatch Institute, "civilization will come to an end."

The statistics, unfortunately, are sleep-inducing: At least 700 million people (some say 1 billion), or one hundred times the population of Denmark, do not have sufficient food to meet energy and protein requirements for a productive, healthy life.

The food shortage for Africa will be 250 million tons by 2020, or twenty times the current food gap. Agricultural production in most African countries has declined since 1970. World Bank estimates indicate that it could take forty years for some African countries to reach their level of food production prior to independence. These estimates do not take into account the agricultural decimation wrought by Rwanda's civil war.

Food production, which increased at an impressive rate in the developing world during the 1980s, has since failed to keep pace with population growth in two-thirds of all developing countries—and in more than 80 percent of African nations.

Meanwhile, internal conflicts, so vividly exemplified by the one in Rwanda, have sent refugee numbers soaring from 8.5 million in 1980 to 23 million by the close of 1994, two-thirds in the developing world. The Rwanda debacle alone resulted in a waterborne cholera catastrophe unprecedented in our century.

Middle East Food Alarm

The Middle East has the world's fastest-growing food deficit. By the end of the century, the region's food demand will create the largest shortfall in the developing world.

Sudan, better known for its killing fields and man-induced famine, was once expected to fill the region's food gap. Arab development groups funneled billions of petrodollars in the 1970s into the "new" breadbasket of the Arab world. By mid-1994, however, Sudanese were growing food in cemeteries.

Food security had become an Arab obsession by the 1980s. Early in that decade, the Arab Organization for Agricultural Development (AOAD) hurriedly produced a voluminous plan for 153 projects at a cost of $33 billion, to be completed by the year 2000. A top Arab official referred to the plan as a "study in futility." Few projects advanced beyond the written page.[1]

Arab food imports jumped from $1.7 billion a year in 1972 to $12.7 billion in 1982. Egypt was importing over 45 percent of its food needs by this time, Jordan more than 50 percent, Libya 60 percent, and Saudi Arabia 75 percent. By the early 1990s, moreover, imports were filling more than 90 percent of Persian Gulf–state food requirements.

Mideast food demand will be twice the 1980 level by 2000. Sixty percent of the increased demand will derive from population growth, and the rest from the growth in per-capita income.[2]

Sudan was food–self-sufficient and even had an export surplus in 1970. But this "food-first" policy ran counter to the wishes of its creditors. Western lenders demanded larger farms, which created an elite landowning class. The

World Bank insisted that Sudan grow cotton for export, and use the earnings to buy foreign food.[3]

The health effects of food insecurity were aptly described to a colleague by a former director of the Food Institute of Egypt: "In the past, children died at an early age due to disease. We have since eliminated many diseases, but it is harder to give the children proper food at an early age. Therefore, we are now producing a lot of idiot children who remain alive to be cared for by society."

Considering Egypt's current population of 58 million people, which is growing by 1 million per year, one can understand why that country's Ministry of Agriculture was renamed the Ministry of Agriculture and Food Security in 1987. Agriculture is Egypt's largest employer, yet the nation imports almost half of its food needs, at a cost of $4 billion in 1990. Egypt's wheat consumption is among the highest in the world.

Where Have All the Farmers Gone?

The obstacles to regional food security are daunting. Mideast food production is beset by acute shortages: of water in Jordan, Israel, the West Bank and Gaza, Iran, and the North African countries; of arable land in Egypt, the Persian Gulf countries, and Lebanon; of labor in Libya and the gulf countries; and of capital in Sudan, Egypt, Syria, Morocco, and Tunisia.

Many Mideast nations relied too long on foreign aid and food imports to supplement domestic production, while they simultaneously encouraged population growth. Looming food deficits now threaten the sociopolitical stability of the entire region.

Countries short of skilled farmers, land, or water could of course invest their capital in nations where land and labor are relatively abundant, such as Syria, Sudan, and Morocco —which, in turn, could invite migrants from other Arab countries, or from Israel, to settle their land and farm it on a permanent basis. While this idea is theoretically worthy, the prospect that Syria will invite Israelis or Turks to settle its land is farfetched in the extreme. Yet the Middle East region will require one-fourth of the world's cereal supply by the year 2000. Who will supply it, and at what cost?[4]

Farmers will not be able to keep up with the expected doubling of world population between 1995 and 2025. Yes, they increased world food production by 3 percent a year between 1950 and 1984, and grain exports by more than 40 percent in the same period. But suddenly, in 1984, they lost momentum. By 1992, per-capita grain harvests and exports had fallen below the 1984 level.

If you are still awake, let me tell you more: The world's croplands began shrinking in 1980. Within a decade, we were pushing against grazing limits throughout the world. The growth of the world beef and mutton production from grasslands was coming to an end.

Future demands for protein-producing agriculture will be satisfied by farming of pork, poultry, and fish. But the world fish catch is flat and the per-capita supply is down.

Fertilizer was the engine driving international food output over the four preceding decades. But how much more fertilizer can the world profitably employ? Plant benefits reached a limit in some cities by the early 1990s, and thereafter began to decline. American fertilizer use in 1992 was below the 1982 level.

The world continues to depend on fertilizers, and on pesticides as a weapon against the pests which can destroy up to 80 percent of a nation's crops, even after harvest. But most of the fertilizer is simply washed away, and the land becomes poorer as a result. The introduction of slow-release fertilizers provides a limited weapon against an awesome opponent: hunger.

Reaching Supply Limits

"The 12-nation European Community spends $63,000 an hour to store 1.4 million tons of unsold butter in refrigerated warehouses," wrote *Time* magazine on September 8, 1993, and "Thais . . . are so angry about subsidized American rice exports that a Bangkok newspaper ran the headline "BEST FRIEND U.S. CUTS THAILAND'S THROAT."

In the United States and Western Europe, high price supports and subsidies encourage farmers to grow bigger crops than markets can absorb. The EC's stockpile of unsold farm goods is valued at over $10.2 billion. The annual wine surplus could fill fifteen hundred Olympic-size swimming pools.

If this seems to contradict the notion that the world faces a food emergency, please read on. From the beginnings of agriculture until the mid–twentieth century, most of the growth in world food output derived from expanding cultivated areas.

Irrigated areas supply more than 50 percent of world food. Three-fourths of all irrigated land is within the developing world, and 60 percent is devoted to production of food grains. Harvested rice consumes over a third, or 70 million hectares. Wheat accounts for 17 percent; fodder, 10 percent; vegetables and fruit, 8 percent; cotton, 7 percent; sugarcane, 6 percent; and maize, 4 percent.

From 1950 to 1978, the food potential of irrigated areas far exceeded the needs of world population. The gains of the Green Revolution—the growing of more food in the same acreage—derived from irrigation. But irrigation is constrained by population growth, aging systems, and the deleterious effect on the environment, including damaged water tables, fisheries, and water-supply systems.

After 1978, per-capita irrigated lands diminished by about 8 percent a year. In Egypt, where all arable land is irrigated, urban spread consumes as much as thirty thousand hectares of cultivable land each year.

Agricultural waters account for nearly 70 percent of worldwide water use. However, over 50 percent of agricultural water is consumed by the very crops we produce, and is therefore unavailable for reuse. Irrigated agriculture, practiced on about 15 percent of all cultivated lands, is the largest drain on all water reserves; it uses more than industrial and domestic water supplies combined.

Man-induced environmental threats vastly compound the food scarcity problem. Soil erosion leads to the loss of land fertility each year, while air pollution decreases annual harvests. Each 1-percent increase in ultraviolet rays means a 1-percent decrease in soybean output, along with stunted plants. Even spray cans for underarm deodorant will have noticeably affected crop output by the year 2020.

With no technological revolution in sight to dramatically raise crop yields in the face of vanishing water supplies, how can Harrison Ford rescue us from the crisis?

The highest-yielding rice varieties, for example, were released twenty-eight years ago. "We can redesign plants so they're more efficient," said Lester Brown, "but we're stuck with photosynthesis."[5]

The time lag between investment in agricultural research

and economic impact can range between three to fifteen years. Even if there were a technological fix, "we would have to make an investment in it now," warned Per Pinstrup-Andersen, director general of the International Food Policy Research Institute. "We can't just sit back on our hands and wait for technological developments to present themselves."[6]

But wait! Isn't there a small country in the Middle East still capable of spearheading agricultural breakthroughs, a country that once turned a denuded wasteland into a paradise of oranges, mangoes, and olives—the last arid land in the world where the desert area is not increasing?

With the moon descending toward a bare, flat horizon, Harrison Ford's last hope of finding the Holy Grain is in one of the smallest Middle Eastern countries. Yet, as act four begins, with the music mounting, he discovers that . . .

6

THE DESERT MAY NOT BLOOM HERE ANYMORE:

Israel

For the Lord your God is bringing you into a good land, a land with streams and springs and fountains issuing from plain and hill; a land of wheat and barley, of vines, figs, and pomegranates, a land of olive trees and honey; a land where you may eat food without stint, where you will lack nothing.

—Deuteronomy 8:7

The future of agriculture in Israel is real estate. The latest mantra within government circles, amongst the children and grandchildren of the Labor Zionists who plowed the land and made the desert bloom, is: "Why should we bother growing our own food? We can buy everything we need from abroad."

Indeed, the internal war between those who believe in relative food self-sufficiency and those who hope to eliminate agriculture altogether is one of Israel's few well-kept secrets. Israel's agricultural sector is an efficiently planned system. Government economists, however, intend to preside over its dismantlement.

Just as Israeli academics and economists are busily attacking planned agriculture, opting instead for Milton Friedman's model of a free-market economy, Palestinians are secretly hoping to organize their agricultural sector according to the highly planned Israel model, including oversight by a board of production. The Palestinian Economic Planning Committee also declared, in July 1994, that it was opposed to economic cooperation with Israel until Palestinian rights were fully achieved.

Cheap Palestinian labor poses the gravest danger to Israeli agriculture. The Israeli economy is based on high technology, sophisticated industry, and low labor costs. The average monthly public-sector salary is six hundred dollars. To keep it this low requires low-priced food—even if it means importing it at a lower price. Food costs were still almost 30 percent of spendable income in 1992.

"Agriculture in Israel is over. People cannot make money. The idea is to turn agricultural lands into a tourist attraction," stated Uri Marinov, a leading environmentalist and former director general of the Ministry of the Environment.[1]

Israeli economists contend that small farms are inefficient. Yet the German government has concluded just the opposite: small farms are an inexpensive way to preserve open spaces and oxygen.

Proper agricultural activity can, at minimum, lead to the preservation of arable lands for future generations, as opposed to the covering of those lands with irreversible concrete, asphalt, and iron. Strangulation could well be the future of the green lungs of the Promised Land.

"Please, for God's sake, give the coming generations the

option of committing their own mistakes. We don't have to perform all their mistakes for them by covering the seashore with a megalopolis," the burly former water commissioner, Meir Ben-Meir, told this writer in June 1994. "At least don't be so arrogantly confident about your proposals.

"Our choices are not between good and bad, but between bad and worse," stated Ben-Meir, a man highly regarded for his knowledge, commitment, and candor. "If my mistake is preserving arable land, and your mistake is using it, my mistake is at least reversible. Yours is not."

Diverting Israel's Agriculture to Latifundia

Israeli officials argue that food security is no longer a problem. What if they are wrong? The 1.2 million acres of arable land in Israel, 20 percent of the country, will be lost to coming generations.

"I oppose diverting the agricultural system of Israel to latifundia," stated an Israeli farmer, referring to the Roman practice of controlling distant land holdings through the enforced servitude of the farmers. Israeli agricultural imports, 11 percent of total imports, were at $1.3 billion in 1992.

Israelis, Palestinians, and Jordanians all hope to meet major food requirements from world imports. Unfortunately, when one deals with strategic planning—which means a period of at least twenty-five years—the primary assumption must be uncertainty. No one could have forecast what would happen in the Soviet Union a year before it occurred.

Israeli agriculture has slowly been moving from the wet

north into the dry southern areas, due to urbanization. Farmers in the south, benefiting from the dry, warm winter, achieve crop production that few other countries can achieve during these cold months. But the Israeli government does not look upon the Negev as a breadbasket.

Although 50 percent of the food produced in the Negev is exported, farmers there are engaged in a continuous struggle for research funds. Farmers and agricultural scientists (only three thousand in number) receive between 20 to 40 percent of their research budget from government sources.

Further progress in increasing yields depends on the use of brackish and deep well water under difficult conditions. The Nubian sandstone aquifer underlying the Negev is fossilized water, laced with epsom salts and gypsum.

Although Israeli scientists have demonstrated that these "bitter" waters can indeed nurture selected crops (strains of wheat, tomatoes, even watermelons and cucumbers), no one is yet certain just how much water can be utilized without endangering or destroying the aquifer. (An aquifer is an underground geological formation supplying water.) Once depleted, it cannot be replenished.

Exporting Know-How

From a rational viewpoint, it seems extraordinary to develop agriculture in semiarid Israel. "But since Israel did produce agriculture for its people, it would be stupid not to make use of the know-how," said Colette Serruya, chief scientist of the Negev region. Israel, she maintained, should work in agriculture in association with other countries that have cheap land, water, and manpower.[2]

Born and raised in France, Serruya has a doctorate in the

hydrological science of lakes and limnology. A student of yoga, she is a handsome woman, athletically thin with brown eyes and gray-streaked black hair that cuts across her forehead. Serruya accepted the job as head of research and development for the Negev because "these were people I could not find in Tel Aviv, with strong dedication. What it takes one year to do in Tel Aviv takes one week in the Negev. I guess the people who live here are the result of natural selection."

Israel's Ministry of Finance believes that agriculture will not exist in the next twenty years, Serruya confirmed. "If so, the know-how developed will be lost. Israel is teaching many countries how to develop alternative agriculture. But if we don't go on with agriculture in this country, we will not have the research potential to help others improve their situation."

Agricultural research is an investment in infrastructure, not less than roads, and it minimizes dependency on outside sources. If the government maintains its policy of limiting investment in agricultural research, how long can Israel maintain its technical advantage?

Even with her dedication to organic crops, Serruya admits that Israeli farmers throughout the rest of the country have been taught to strive for higher yields. A different mind-set could be more easily molded in the Negev-Arava, she believes, given the relative isolation.

However, if the peace process succeeds, the people of the area may someday long for isolation from an explosion in tourism and related business concerns. "The Negev will become the most sought after tourist area you have ever seen in your life. Combined with the coast of Saudi Arabia, the Sinai, and Aqaba, the French Riviera will be nothing compared to it," Serruya commented.

The Jordanian peace agenda had initially included the

"return" of a 380-square-kilometer area along the Arava riverbed linking the Dead Sea and the Gulf of Eilat—"disputed" lands that were left fallow by Jordan and developed by Israel with Jordan's "tacit" consent. But this highly fertile land, and the water it holds, is a matter of survival for Arava farmers and residents, who would be forced to rely on less fertile soil and less water if they lost the right to farm there.

"It's an awkward situation. We haven't been told anything. We know it will affect our land, but have no idea how much and where. We're not hysterical, but we're definitely worried," noted Ido Zvulun of Kibbutz Lotan, prior to the signing of the Israeli-Jordan Peace Agreement of July 26, 1994.[3]

"We depend on agriculture for our existence," he continued. "At least 80 percent of our income is from farming, and there's not alternative cultivable area which hasn't already been located and utilized. The water problem is critical, too. Even if all the fantastic plans for joint water desalination plants get under way, what happens in the meantime, during the next 15 years."

Amotz Rubin from Moshav Idan in the northern Arava stressed that "the Jordanians are claiming 100 percent of our farmlands. We would be left with just the gardens by our homes." Rubin has spent twenty years in the Arava and "yet I have never seen any Jordanian activities in the area to suggest that this is their land." Nor, he declared, did any government body "tell us that this was disputed territory—not when they gave us grants, loans or helped construct infrastructure."[4]

With further Negev dry-land agriculture constrained by declining soil productivity, the farmers were vastly relieved by Jordan's agreement to forgo its demands for the return of lands in the Arava under the terms of a peace agenda. Even under optimum conditions, sophisticated agriculture can only cover 250,000 dunams of land both in the Negev and throughout the country, or 20 percent of existing irrigated areas.

Israel has been hailed as the only arid country that has managed, until now, to forestall invading desert sands. Over 50 percent of the land area of Israel is an arid or semiarid zone. "If we do not keep the land through agriculture, we will in no time have barren land, a dry and yellow environment. The destruction of agriculture is a magnet for accelerating desertification," Serruya pointed out.[5]

No Future Without Our Past

The highway from Tel Aviv to Jerusalem is typically a plodding traffic jam, where the Messiah himself would have to patiently wait in line. Two-thirds of the way, however, there is a shiny new exit directing the driver to a sparsely traveled bypass. The new road to Jerusalem, through a rolling terrain of trees and hills, is a pathway backward in time. Unspoilt by the mega–shopping centers and high-rise buildings that have gobbled up so much of the Promised Land, here the pristine beauty remains intact.

The sign reading NEOT KEDUMIM is a few miles ahead on the left. The beckoning detour concludes, suddenly, at a majestic tapestry of swaying trees, brilliantly flowering bushes, and hilltops speckled with greenery as far as the eye can see. Neot Kedumim is a biblical garden, containing acres upon acres of the plants and trees of ancient Israel.

The man responsible for restoring this ancient heritage is

Nogah Hareuveni. In a purple shirt and faded jeans, he stands five foot ten, with the sinewy build of a man who prefers walking to food. His thick white hair is streaked with black. The deeply grooved smile suggests a life spent outdoors, yet otherwise his face is strangely free of the ravages of time or weather.

Tree branches hug the window of his office, a small, spare room with desk, file cabinet, and scattered books—and an expansive view of biblical hilltops. He picks up a ringing phone to hear the caller inquire, "How many years has it been since Nogah Hareuveni passed away?"

"I am still very much alive," he replies with glee. Nogah is in his early seventies, and Neot Kedumim is his lifelong dream fulfilled. The inspiration came from his parents, leading botanists in pre-1948 Palestine. "Born into this dream," he spent his entire adulthood "knocking on doors and hearts to make it reality. In 1994, Nogah received the Israel Prize, the government's highest recognition, for this lifetime achievement.

Neot Kedumim was established in 1965 with thirty olive trees transplanted to eroded soil that had been barren for ten thousand years. Broad-branched cedars of Lebanon, seeded from trees 3,000 years old, now cool the landscape.

When Nogah was but a small child, his parents obtained permission from the minister of agriculture of Lebanon to transport cedar cones to Israel for their botanic museum in Jerusalem. Nogah still has a picture of himself standing on the minister's shoulders, picking these treasures. The museum was destroyed during the 1948 war, but the trees survived.

"*Kedem,* in Hebrew, means 'ancient,' while *kadimah* means 'going forward to the sun,' " he explained. "There is no future without our past. We cannot look forward to our future without knowing our past and understanding the basis of our culture."[6]

He looked out the window, speaking so softly that his voice could barely be heard. "I try to discern what the Bible wants us to understand in the name of God," he said. "Take the very expression, *Shmah Yisrael . . . Adonay Echad,* 'Hear oh Israel, God is One.' The Hebrew root of *Shmah—shin, mem, ayin*—conveys 'hearing,' but even more so 'understanding.'

"When Solomon was anointed king, God asked him, 'What shall I give you?' Solomon, after all, was the son of quite a poor king, David, the shepherd. So how did Solomon later become a very rich king? He didn't ask God for money or power, but asks in Hebrew, 'Give me an understanding heart.' The heart was believed to be the source of wisdom."

Monotheism, Nogah emphasized, is a way of belief. The Hebrew prayer words *Adonai Echad* translate as "oneness" or "unity" in the whole of creation. But there is a difference between believing that there is one God and "actually understanding it," Nogah said. The challenge for the prophets of Israel was to teach the people to understand the concept of oneness.

Religious definitions of Jewishness, in Nogah's view, are "nonsense." The one common denominator to all Jews and also to Christians is the relationship between the land and the Bible. Neot Kedumim illuminates the hidden ties between the land of the Bible and the people. Nogah concludes, provocatively, that "there are no ties at all, because the land and people, our culture and ideas, were in fact created as one body.

"You can have ties between two bodies. But the land,

the belief, and the culture are interlaced. This is the secret of how the Jewish people were established," he stressed. "The borders can change, the political status can change, and does from time to time—sometimes after years, or decades, or centuries. But these changes cannot affect the one body and heritage which comprises the people and the land of Israel."

The menorah, national emblem of Israel, is rooted in the land. The flame symbolizes the light of the olive tree and its oil, "a light unto the world." The mezuzah, a precise Hebrew parchment placed on the doorpost of Jewish homes, refers to both the problems of water and the key crops in ancient Israel: grain, wine, and oil. The grain represents wheat and barley, the two most problematic crops, whereas the most crucial challenge facing the farmer was rain.

Once he had harvested them, the farmer or shepherd was required by the nation's priests and spiritual leaders to bring his grain, wine, and oil to Solomon's Temple, created for the purpose of worshiping one God. Through this experience, they understood that the world is not divided or controlled by forces that fight with each other. On the contrary, there is balance in nature, to which man must adapt.

The Talmud teaches that since the temple was destroyed, the table in a Jewish home replaces the temple altar. The challah bread (flour), the candles (olive oil flames), and the ever-present wine (grapes) symbolize the most crucial and problematic crops of ancient Israel.

"If there is no flour, there is no Torah; if there is no Torah, there is no flour," said Rabbi Elazar ben Azaria, a third-century sage. The material depends upon the spiritual, and the spiritual upon the material. The bounty of the harvest is conditional upon "paying heed to the commandments that I give you this day" (Deut. 11:13).

Kindergarten children who visit Neot Kedumim participate in the plowing of the land. They sow their own seeds and ask for rain. The same children return to harvest their crop. "You should see," said Nogah, "how each of them knows exactly where his or her seed is planted."

The ripened sheaves were attacked recently by fungi during a year of overly abundant rainfall. "If, as a four-year-old child, you go to harvest your own crop, but cry over the sheave that is black, or if you study how to separate the grain, how to make the flour, and then read from the Talmud the words of a rabbi describing the first tasks on earth that man had to engage in to obtain bread . . . just imagine the effect!

"The children discover that these are not just black letters written in the pages of the Bible. We feel the life of the land of our forefathers, and from this we understand our heritage," he said.

Israel's ancestors saw nothing wrong with using the features of the land, Nogah said, "so long as the balance in nature was protected." Isaiah spoke about the highways that would be made for the people—"every valley would rise up and every mountain would go down"—in order to make a road for exiles returning to Jerusalem.

"Our culture can bring back the land to its original balance," Nogah emphasized. But what are the consequences if people do not pay heed to the ancient dicta regarding the water, land, and environment? "I do not even want to think about the consequences," he said. "Today, it could lead to catastrophe."

7

ISRAELIS AND PALESTINIANS:
Storing Water for the Dry Years Ahead

The primary weapons in the global battle against galloping desertification are agriculture, or trees and parks—which also consume substantial water. Current Israeli development plans, however, envision a continuous town from Haifa to Ashdod, with only small national parks in between. The government, believing the coastal area should be urbanized, has so far demonstrated little understanding of the potential ecological disaster.

The underlying coastal aquifer is the largest of Israel's three sources of water. If the area is covered by concrete, rainfall will flood into the Mediterranean, instead of replenishing the water supply. Destruction of an aquifer is prevented both by managing withdrawals in such a way as to preserve the integrity of the aquifer, and by ensuring that land use allows rainfall to percolate into the aquifer. The latter can best be accomplished through the maintenance of agriculture or through the establishment of parks.

"If you build atop the coastal aquifer, there will be no

opportunity to recharge the aquifer. This is the largest aquifer we have; no other can store for a period of a few years," Colette Serruya noted.

But government officials believe the least expensive way to absorb newcomers and army personnel is by building in the central region, from Ashdod to Naharia. Roughly 70 percent of Israel's population already resides within fifteen kilometers of the Mediterranean coastline. The coastal aquifer, in short, is most endangered by economists and city planners.

The freshwater Sea of Galilee and the mountain aquifer (Yarkon Tananim) also offer storage capacity. Palestinians contend that the mountain aquifer belongs to them. Territory and water are one. But without access to sufficient storage capacity, Palestinians cannot avoid a severe water shortage in twenty to twenty-five years.

✦ ✦ ✦

Neither Israel, Israeli Arabs, nor the Palestinians of the West Bank and Gaza possess sufficient water storage capacity to bridge the dry years ahead.

Both lakes and aquifers can serve as reservoirs; water can be stored there in a rainy year, to be pumped out at a later time as needed. In 1991, however, the Israeli government allowed so much water to be pumped from the Sea of Galilee (a freshwater lake), that the sea dropped to a dangerously low level, where it was threatened with contamination by underlying saline springs.

Any proposal for new sources of water (generally more expensive than current sources) that ignores the recovery of the coastal aquifer is, in effect, relinquishing a cheap resource and opting for the more expensive. Conversely, any proposal that fails to deal with the coastal aquifer should be charged with its loss, as well as with the loss of the storage capacity provided by the aquifer. Both are quantifiable.

Scarcity of water storage capacity in the Promised Land is as significant as the lack of rainfall and the drought cycle. In 1992, following the three-year period of drought, Israel benefited from a very rainy year. But most of the water flooded into the Dead Sea or the Mediterranean.

In 1993, also a rainy year, flooding into the Mediterranean was even higher, due to both a lack of capacity to pump water fast enough, and a lack of storage capacity. In short, there was no room to store water in 1993.

The Israeli-Jordanian proposal for a man-made canal linking the Red Sea with the Dead Sea is based on the argument that sufficient electricity would be generated to desalinate seawater and provide additional freshwater so urgently needed by Jordan, Israel, and the Palestinians. But where will the water produced by this canal be stored?

The production of water by desalination will be linear, 365 days per year. Since day and night consumption are not equal, the freshwater produced at night must be stored.

A less costly means of providing storage capacity would be by pumping water out of the Sea of Galilee and through a water canal to other parts of the country. A cubic meter pumped out leaves behind a storage capacity of one cubic meter. In this case, the cost of storage is zero, since the lake already exists. The more water pumped from the Sea of Galilee, the greater the storage capacity.

One proposal under review by the Israeli government is to lay pipelines that will bring seawater to Beth-Shean, across the Jezreel valley. Desalination plants in Beth-Shean would produce freshwater, with approximately half pumped to the Sea of Galilee as a reserve, and the remainder routed to Jordan and to West Bank Palestinians.

The waters pumped into the Sea of Galilee would allow for the diversion of the northern Jordan River directly to the south (before it becomes polluted), providing cleaner water than that available through the National Water Carrier, Israel's network for pumping water from the Sea of Galilee for use throughout the country. The northern Jordan River, however, could be diminished in the process, and no one can foretell the consequences of pumping 2 billion cubic meters of seawater through the width of the country.

The Last Drop of Water

Simulations conducted over recent years demonstrate that the water potential of Israel (the amount of water that the country can withdraw annually from groundwater sources) is between 1.8 and 1.9 billion cubic meters.

The population between the Jordan and the Mediterranean was 7 million people in 1991, approximately 5 million in Israel and 2 million in the West Bank and Gaza. Also in 1991, a year of severe drought, the share of water delivered to Israeli agriculture was reduced by 50 percent of annual consumption.

Let us assume that the population growth of the area continues at 3 percent, including immigration. Based on this scenario, there will be approximately 11 million people living between the Jordan and the Mediterranean by 2015.

In an average year of average rainfall, there will be sufficient drinking water for a future urban civilization of 18 million people, with drinking water use by Israelis and Palestinians equalized. However, at the point when their combined populations reach 11 million—with urban water use by Israelis and Palestinians equalized—another dry cycle could well wreak havoc on the economic conditions and quality of life of both parties.

Since agriculture will have been eliminated as the flexible consumer (that is, the sector where water use can still be reduced and diverted to other priorities), Israelis and Palestinians will be forced to rely *only* on the actual water available in any particular year. "At this point," said Meir Ben-Meir, "Israelis and Palestinians will have exploited their last drop of fresh water."

Charge for the Bath Water— Don't Throw Out the Baby

Israel's comptroller general concluded in 1991 that the continuous decline in the water supply was largely due to the low cost of subsidized water used by the agricultural sector. A high portion of the water was used for export cultivation.

"The hidden water subsidy was in effect passed along to foreign consumers," Miriam Ben Porat emphasized in her annual report; she described the phenomenon as "exporting water at a loss." Most agricultural crops exported from Israel are actually 80 to 90 percent water. "Don't send vegetables to Europe," said a member of the Environmental Ministry, "just send water!"

The comptroller called for a master plan for short- and long-term agricultural developments, and a wise reassessment of the policy of "exporting" water. She did not, it should be emphasized, advocate the elimination of agriculture.

"It is imperative," she stated, "that there be no difference between the price of water for agricultural use and the true cost which the planners face when approving investments in new waterworks meant to increase the supply of water."

Hence, water can be priced at its true cost, which greatly reduces or eliminates the export of water at a loss, without drastically threatening or eliminating agriculture (i.e., throwing out the baby).

While Israel's state comptroller has declared that "it will be impossible to expand agricultural production in the coming years," Palestinians—drawing from the same vanishing pool of water—demand the right to vastly expand their agricultural sector and exports as a key basis of their economy. Left to their own devices, the Palestinians could face insurmountable odds in simply covering the costs of their current drinking water supply, let alone the costs of desalinated water for drinking purposes or for agriculture.

Many Israelis argue that Israel should build a new National Water Carrier in the next ten to fifteen years. But the government has so far failed to put aside the money, which could be raised by charging today's urban water users for the cost of the new alternative carrier.

West Bank Palestinians obtain water through Mekorot, Israel's national water company, for a fee. Israeli authorities have long contended that Israeli settlers and Palestinians in the territories pay the Israeli government equal amounts for water. Palestinians claim that drinking water going to the settlers is subsidized by the Israeli government, and that Israelis are sapping more than their fair share of the waters.

The only issue on which both sides agree is that there will be insufficient freshwater for their respective populations by the first quarter of the next millennium. Given this harsh reality, the cost of using today's vanishing resources should pay the price of tomorrow's alternative water supply.

8

ARMAGEDDON UNDERGROUND?

With Middle East population growth rates averaging a staggering 3 percent, the mere prospect of overflowing sewage could bring Middle Easterners to loggerheads. The annual wastewater collected from the Greater Cairo area alone is equivalent to the total amount of water used for domestic, industrial, and irrigation purposes in Jordan.

Miriam Ben Porat, Israel's comptroller general, reported in May 1994 that residents would be forbidden to drink water in many areas of the country, if the water were evaluated by Western standards. Treatment of water pollution and sewage has shown no "tangible change for the better," she stated.[1]

Responsible ministries have so far failed to produce a national map of water and sewage systems to pinpoint potential sources of pollution, Ben Porat said. Mandatory water testing procedures are typically ignored, or conducted without all the required tests. A policy decision to filter all drinking water by 1997 still lacks financial backing. A central monitoring system of underground water sources is imperative, said the comptroller, as an early warning against pollution of the water table.

The Gaza aquifer is almost completely destroyed. The salt level is so high there that the water is hardly fit for irrigation. In fact, Mekorot has tabled plans to build a desalination plant in Gaza for drinking water.

"People have to understand that keeping their vicinity clean will be the most expensive part of their life," opined Meir Ben-Meir sadly. "Otherwise they will break the very branch they are sitting on. Israel is doing a lot, but certainly not enough. Let us just say that nobody inside of Israel is pleased."[2]

At a Knesset committee hearing on June 1, 1994, Labor Party member Yoram Lass noted that the amount of pollutants permitted in drinking water in Israel is double what it is in Europe. The standards, he suggested, do not appear to be based on any objective criteria.[3]

The coastal aquifer is especially threatened by overpumping and thus by the lowering of the water table—leaving it lower than the sea—which results in salt water seepage into the aquifer. From time to time, the Water Committee of Israel recharges the coastal aquifer with surplus rainwater from the Sea of Galilee. Yet the hydrological deficit in the coastal aquifer in the drought year of 1990 was more than 1 billion cubic meters, and a tremendous deficit still remains.

If the coastal aquifer is not treated and protected, this critical storage source will be lost not only to Israel, but also to the Palestinians and the water-starved Jordanians.

"It is imperative first and foremost to rapidly rehabilitate the coastal aquifer, and to establish . . . effective reserves, as needed," urged the comptroller general. "It will require taking emergency steps—tangibly reducing allocations in the coming decade to increase water levels in the reservoirs to the desired goals. The problem of the pollution of the pure-water aquifers and the Knerret [Sea of Galilee] must be attacked."[4]

Below one of the most intensively used agricultural areas in the world, the coastal aquifer is further embattled by fertilizers, pesticides, landfills, and effluents.

"There is no question that the coastal aquifer is abused," Uri Marinov agreed. "In fact, some people believe we should forget about using it for drinking water and draw upon it only for agriculture. This of course makes the mountain aquifer all the more important."[5]

With a good portion of the pollution still in the soil, and advancing downward, the future will only be worse, unless there is concerted action.

The Final Battle Is Below

Israel's strategic concern in a final resolution of the Palestinian conflict is underground: specifically the Yarkon ("spring") Taninim ("crocodile") mountain aquifer that lies beneath both pre-1967 Israeli territory and the West Bank. What is most remarkable about this aquifer is the lack of consensus concerning its geological description.

West Bank Palestinians are currently receiving per capita one-third to one-fourth of the amount of water that Israel uses. Israel must (and intends to) increase their portion. The question is: From where? The West Bank aquifer is already being used almost to capacity.

Twenty-five percent of Israeli and Palestinian drinking water comes from the Jordan River–Sea of Galilee system, while 75 percent derives from the coastal and mountain aquifers. The mountain aquifer, however, is the main source of drinking water for most of the large cities.

A variety of Israeli, Palestinian, and foreign experts will contend that 80, 60, 40, or 20 percent of the mountain aquifer lies under the West Bank—depending on whom you talk to. There may be more than one truth. Theoretically, 70 to 80 percent of the aquifer is in the West Bank, as well as 70 to 80 percent of the recharged waters. However, all of these recharged waters flow westward toward the coastal plain and the Mediterranean Sea.

Israel pumps the majority of the naturally recharged waters, and has been doing so since the mid-1960s, to sustain its agricultural, industrial, and population growth. The mountain aquifer supplies approximately 40 percent of Israel's agricultural waters and almost 50 percent of its drinking water, while underground resources, wastewater reclamation, catchments, saline springs, and other sources provide the remainder.

Yet both Israeli Jews and Israeli Arabs use more water per capita for domestic purposes than West Bank and Gaza Palestinians. Domestic and industrial use combined, however, account for less than 30 percent of Israel's supply; agriculture is the primary user of water, not only in Israel, but throughout the Middle East. Water-absorbing crops like cotton (greatly reduced over the past few years), have helped ravish the water supply.

Palestinian experts generally acknowledge that Israel provides requisite water to the West Bank for domestic and industrial use. Indeed, one of the first policy actions of the Palestinian authority was to contract with Mekorot to continue supplying water to both Jericho and the Gaza Strip. Palestinians nevertheless claim that Israel refuses sufficient water for agricultural expansion, which is viewed as the linchpin of economic viability for the territories. Israeli authorities respond that agriculture has been the primary culprit in the draining of the aquifer's resources.

The agricultural sector supplies 7 percent of Israel's gross national product, and drains more than 70 percent of the country's water. Israeli farmers were forced to accept a 30-percent and then a 50-percent reduction in water during the 1990–91 drought, while Israelis living in the West Bank were prohibited from engaging in extensive farming.

The water commissioner allowed the mountain aquifer's water levels to drop below the red line in 1990—a highly dangerous gamble. "If the pumping region of the mountain aquifer is salinated, the supply of drinking water to the public will be seriously and irreparably hurt, and serious damage will be caused to the state's economy," declared the state comptroller.[6]

The aquifer has already been exploited to dangerous limits, and overuse or free drilling by either side in the future will exacerbate salinity and result in irreparable damage.

The Sea of Galilee, which supplies almost one-third of Israel's freshwater requirements, was at its lowest level in the past century in 1991. Israel is currently utilizing its water resources at between 15 and 20 percent beyond their natural replenishment rate, causing water table levels to drop and shallow wells to go dry.

In short, the parties to the conflict—Israel, the West Bank and Gaza, and Jordan—are combatants in quicksand, facing a combined water deficit of 300 to 400 million cubic meters per year, which is aggravated by drought conditions and water salinity.

The Gaza Strip, 50 percent desert, claims only one aquifer. Contamination there has already reached a critical level, due to the heavy local use of pesticides and fertilizers, and the lack of services to remove or treat raw sewage in many towns and villages. Overpumping has also caused seawater intrusion, and the aquifer's salinity quotient is continually rising. Gaza's water will be unusable by the year 2000, when its population will number 1 million.

Remember King David's Tsinnor?

He who controls the water channels of the Promised Land rules the country.

Water from the mountain aquifer water is pumped from wells within Israel's pre-1967 borders, but every drop enters the aquifer system from the high ground of Judea and Samaria. As gravity draws the water west, north, and south toward the Israeli wells, its volume is diminished by pumping along the way, according to Itamar Marcus, chairman of the Movement for the Preservation of Israel's Water.[7]

"Whoever controls the pumps in Judea and Samaria determines the amount of water left to flow across the Green Line," Marcus wrote. The state comptroller reported in May 1989 that "the physical capability exists to increase pumping in Judea and Samaria to a degree that will completely eliminate pumping in Israel."[8]

Palestinian negotiators demand 100 percent of the water entering the ground in the West Bank. They also demand compensation for water pumped since 1948, or at minimum, since 1967. Based on this scenario, and without desalinated or imported water, Israel could face a catastrophe. Agriculture would be destroyed and the green revolution reversed.

During the 1991 crisis, just to reduce water usage by a few percentage points, the government limited the watering of gardens, raised water prices, reduced water to agriculture, and touted water conservation as a national priority.

"What life in this country would be like . . . is beyond imagination," Marcus stressed. "It would affect not just our life-style but our very psyche as a nation. Ecologically, residents of the coastal plain would be at the mercy of the residents of the high lands of Judea and Samaria."[9]

The Palestinians also hope to spur immigration of at least 1 million refugees, and have earmarked a major portion of their international financial aid for expansion of agricultural development in competition with Israeli farmers, and for industrial infrastructure. (The West Bank–Gaza birth rate is seven to eight children per woman, as compared to two to three among Israeli Arabs.)

Industrial waste from the autonomous regions could severely damage Israel's water supply. Rami Gabizon, an expert on water with the state comptroller's office, told a Knesset committee on June 1, 1994, that waste from Palestinian industries in the Judean hills could pollute all the underground reservoirs in the region. He criticized the Israeli peace negotiating team for paying insufficient attention to this matter. Meanwhile, water commissioner Gideon Tzur described the threat as "cardinal" and "critical." If Palestinians did not take steps to prevent this nightmare from becoming reality, Tzur declared, it could even be sufficient reason to break the agreement with the PLO.[10]

"We have the right to develop our resources in water, to dig wells in Gaza and Jericho," Jamil Tarifi, head of the PLO's negotiating team on civilian issues, told his Israeli counterparts. "There is total Palestinian authority. There is no limit to our authority."[11]

The mountain aquifer, which has suffered less from economic activity, is much cleaner and has a better quality of water than the coastal aquifer. But it is also more sensitive to pollution. As most of the aquifer lies under a rock formation, pollution can quickly penetrate. The coastal aquifer, by contrast, is sandy, and therefore contaminants must travel years, as opposed to days or weeks, to reach it.

Any group or people living above an aquifer and not treating their sewage is polluting that aquifer with nutrients, salt, chemicals, heavy metals, and viruses. If the Palestinians residing in the West Bank are unable to treat all of their sewage, the mountain aquifer will be critically endangered. Presently, more than 50 percent of the sewage in the territories is untreated.

Sewage from Nablus and other towns is already forming noxious brown rivers of untreated household waste. Flowing west, it seeps into Israel's aquifers. Today, Tel Aviv's water is clean only because the population in Judea and Samaria is limited, so that the environment is able to filter out the pollutants that enter the ecosystem there. With several hundred million dollars being pumped into Palestinian industry and agriculture, the flood of waste flowing to the coast could bring ecological disaster.

Geologist Professor Arnon Sofer of Haifa University, one of Israel's foremost water experts and an adviser to the Ministry of Foreign Affairs, has warned that, without proper waste management, a million more Arabs will "finish off the Israeli coast with sewage, dysentery, and typhus."[12]

Overpumping in the West Bank could eventually lower the water table below sea level, causing salt water to flow from the sea into Israel's coastlands. This could lead to permanent destruction of aquifers and farmland.

In practical terms, Israel could secure its water future by permanently maintaining control over the three West Bank regions where pumping affects the water flow to Israeli wells. Comprising 20 percent of the land, these regions rest adjacent to the Green Line in northern and western Samaria, and include the Jerusalem hills heading south past Gush Etzion.

The political train, however, appears to be moving in the opposite direction. The Israel–PLO agreement of September 1993 led to the creation of a Palestinian water authority in Gaza and Jericho, where Palestinians now have the right to dig as many wells as they wish. But at what cost and what threat to the water below? And what will happen to the underground water supply as the autonomous region expands throughout the West Bank?

9

THE GATE OF NO RETURN:

From Israel to Jordan

For all at last returns to the sea—to Oceanus, the ocean river, like that ever-flowing stream of time, the beginning of the end.

—Rachel Carson,
Silent Spring, 1962

"I'm so free, I can do what I want to do." The song pounded through gigantic speakers straight to the heavens. It was one o'clock in the morning on the moonlit beach of Eilat's Dolphin Reef.

Yellow, blue, and white lights sparkled far across the waters in Aqaba, a sweet stage setting on the Jordanian side of the Gulf. The jutting tip of Saudi Arabia was faintly visible in the distance.

Empowered by the dancing, swishing water, the mass of people was undulating, gyrating, hands in air—one big body swaying, jumping, party to an ancient rite of joy. Sandy dust rose from beneath their feet into little billowy clouds that disappeared through rainbow strobe lights toward the half moon above.

They trust each other, I thought. They have no fear. These dancers in their oneness are an extended family in a large neighborhood of differences. Familiarity even amongst strangers.

Though I was alone, I decided to join in the celebration. It was easy to blend in, for the line between couples and individuals had blurred. At the water's edge of Israel and Jordan, with the sandy mountains for protection, I too felt free, and wide awake.

Finding a Place in Our Own Creation

Ronnie Zilber, the owner of the Dolphin Reef, smiled disarmingly, brown eyes squinting; he proffered a home-style brew of easy banter. Six feet tall, with a thin strong build, deeply tanned, he was wearing purple shorts and a faded blue shirt the day we met.

Zilber spent many years residing in a trailer caravan in the Sinai, catching tropical Red Sea fish for sale for family aquariums. His partner was the infamous Rafi Eitan, who —when he wasn't busy serving as a master spy—was making fishy connections to the rest of the world.

I had come to interview him about his dolphins and about pollution threats to the Gulf of Eilat (or the Gulf of Aqaba as it is called by the Jordanians). The waters are calm and deep, but very narrow and delicate. Everything put into the water remains there, just as in a swimming pool.

"People think they can drop anything into the water without consequence," Zilber noted. While Israeli and

Jordanian residents are beginning to understand the consequences of their actions, "the distance between understanding and doing could lead to a gate of no return," he said. "When you think about losing the beauty, you must think green. Today we cannot find a place for ourselves in our own creation."

He continued: "We see it by the reduction of corals and algae in the northern part of the gulf. The reduced clarity of the water means that less sun rays are penetrating and therefore there are less corals at certain depths."

Minerals mined from the Dead Sea by Israel and Jordan, then turned into fertilizer, are brought to Eilat/Aqaba to be loaded on ships. But much of the fertilizer disappears with the wind, and settles in the water. Fertilizer creates new breeds of algae, which alters the water's ecological balance.

In this regard, lingering disagreements between Jordan and Israel are akin to an argument between two people on a bus, both fighting over a single seat, while the bus is hurtling toward a cliff. Now that secret-but-cold peace between Jordan and Israel is rapidly warming, the parties must ask, "Where is the bus headed?"

Recycled sewage both from the cities of Eilat and Aqaba, and from hotels along the shore, even if free of bacteria, is nevertheless "freshwater being poured into seawater," which further affects the indigenous algae. Although the Gulf of Eilat may appear clean from the surface, the worst pollution lies tucked beneath its carpet of many colors.

A ship from Bangkok, for example, arrives in Eilat or Aqaba seemingly empty. Yet a big ship can never sail unloaded, since this reduces speed. Therefore the tanker travels to Bangkok, unloads its goods, sucks the water from the harbor inside its belly, and finally deposits the water in the Red Sea waters of Eilat.

When an animal is brought into the area, it naturally undergoes medical checks and immunization. But there are virtually no constraints against ships bringing in foreign bacteria or viruses, when, for instance, "100,000 cubic meters of the most polluted water in the world is taken from one harbor and dropped into the Red Sea." Zilber pointed out that ships suck in small animals as well, "but no one talks about it or even sees it." The trail of deadly waste left behind also kills the dolphins. The Gulf of Eilat once boasted a major population of dolphins, but today fewer come for shorter visits.

The concept of a "Red Sea Riviera" evolving from peaceful economic relations between Israel and Jordan is an exhilarating prospect (MAKE TOURISM, NOT WAR, stated an Israeli magazine headline). But a building frenzy of more hotels along the shore, without utmost concern for the environmental consequences of expanding refuse, could sully the waters of Aqaba and Eilat beyond redemption.

The water gate between Israel and Jordan can lead to an enduring cooperation, or to the erosion of the water jewel they share, if special care is not taken and preventive investments are not made by all partners to peace.

Underwater Ballet

The dolphin is the only nondomesticated animal that purposely seeks out the company of human beings without primary reinforcement.

Why is the dolphin attracted to human beings? And what do we have to offer? Zilber discounts all commonplace theories. He established the Dolphin Reef on the principle of the dolphin's "unexplained attitude toward human beings."

Most dolphinariums turn their dolphins into pet acrobats, rewarding prowess with tasty morsels. Zilber does just the opposite. He explained his philosophy with the following analogy: "I have a little daughter who likes to kiss me, and I thought, how could I cause her to kiss me more? Perhaps I should give her a candy each time? Then I realized that my daughter will look at the kiss as the means to get the candy, and I will ruin the kiss.

"First of all, it will be just a means to get something else. And each time I forget to buy candy in the market, I will have to chance giving up the kiss—or she may stop liking the candy, and I will get no kiss.

"So all over the world, the dolphin is looking at you as a means to get dolphin candy, which is exactly what ruins our communication." Consequently, Zilber's dolphins receive neither reinforcement nor punishment. "This is not a philosophy," he said, "this is a reality."

In order to help the dolphins understand that their abilities are recognized and respected, Zilber not only regularly opens the gate to the Red Sea, but actually forces the dolphins to leave their protected area—to which they always return of their own volition. The dolphins, which live between twenty to thirty years under positive conditions, seem content.

Zilber also recently brought nine blackfoot penguins to the Dolphin Reef, hoping that by watching how penguins survive in water, he could better understand the dolphin. "I live next to the water, and I breathe air," he noted, "therefore air-breathing animals are of special interest to me."

The penguin, who breathes air and likes to be in the water, is one of the least intelligent animals on earth. Having virtually no brain, a penguin acts largely on instinct. "The penguin doesn't have to think in order to make decisions; he is computerized by God," Zilber pointed out. "But the dolphin—like mankind—must think whether or not to take food, to play now or later, and to be nice to this person or not."

The dolphins especially enjoy playing with the penguins, grabbing them by the legs and tossing them like a basketball.

What Is the Dolphin Trying to Tell Us?

No one likes the prospect of being rejected by a dolphin. Think about it. You're given a magic opportunity to swim with dolphins in crisp Red Sea waters. You are told, however, that the dolphins may or may not choose to swim close to you. You are also made aware that dolphins will rush to the side of a handicaped or abused child, an adult suffering from an untreatable affliction or pain, and to certain people.

What does it take to be chosen by a dolphin? Must one be sufficiently vulnerable or open? Can the dolphin see into our hearts? Suddenly, the goal is transformed. "Not being rejected" by a dolphin is no longer a sufficient condition. A fluttering hope suddenly arises that the dolphins will actually "like" you.

The British government sent a group of abused children to Dolphin Reef. These previously angry, withdrawn, and bitter children returned home smiling and happy. Why? In the relationship between human beings and animals, there is no more empathic connection than between man and dolphin. The dolphins demonstrate an uncanny ability to identify and understand those who most need their nurturing skills.

At Dolphin Reef, there have been many cases of incredible and inexplicable healing sessions. A physically immobile child that had never before moved even his head or arm was suddenly able to turn his entire body by himself after swimming with the dolphins. An autistic child who had been unable to utter even a simple phrase was suddenly able to do so after hugging a dolphin. The small boy, who had previously refused to make eye contact with his parents, let alone show affection, is now spontaneously touching and kissing his mother and father.

A woman in the depths of depression was nursed out of her despair by two dolphins. A stroke victim who had not spoken to his wife in months rediscovered his will to communicate; a child with cancer and deformed neck muscles departed from the dolphin with his head completely straight for the very first time. And for others, the dolphin seems to provide a reason to live.

Confronting the dolphin's ever-sweet smile, few can remain impassive. Indeed, the dolphin may be purposely trying to reveal its nurturing and psychic abilities.

The dolphin's brain is twenty times larger, relative to body weight, than man's. The dolphin lets only half of its brain sleep at any given time, and is therefore always conscious of his environment—unlike the human being, who spends almost a third to half of life in an unconscious state.

Could the dolphin's heart be more empathic than that of man, as well?

And why has it taken humans more than five thousand years to "accidentally" reach such conclusions about this air-breathing mammal? Previous civilizations may have had awareness of and appreciation for the dolphin—and its relationship to both mankind and water—that were lost over time.

Naomi, a trained nurse from South Africa and my dive instructor, extolled the joys and humor of her new life in the company of dolphins. Tanned and trim, she was wearing a pink bathing suit underneath the black rubbery diving garb. I watched transfixed from beneath the blue as she played with Cindy, her favorite male, who especially liked to be stroked on the back of his tail. The mammal placed his head on Naomi's shoulder and even allowed Naomi to hug him. "Dolphins can serve as our healers and as a sensor for our internal beings," said Naomi. "But instead we kill them."

Singing songs we have not yet understood, these intelligent, gentle, and wise creatures signal commands to each other for underwater ballet. Perhaps dolphin are also trying to alert us to a dimension and quality of life that we are not ready to comprehend. "We humans have a purpose on this earth," said another trainer. "Dolphins are the same."

The halo of sunset was settling over the Dolphin Reef when I departed from these waters and from the dolphins. Within the power circles of Washington, petting an animal would not be regarded as a particularly meaningful achievement. But in the Red Sea waters between Israel and Jordan, I felt that by the very act of stroking the velvety skin of a dolphin, sleek and cool, I was actually making a contribution to the universe. Perhaps it is no coincidence that these ethereal creatures inhabit this spiritual gateway to lasting peace.

Abraham's Child: Jordan

In the Royal Palace a senior Jordanian official confided to this writer fears that his country would disappear in less than ten years if water disputes with Syria in particular, and Israel in general, were not defused in the near future.

The Hashemite Kingdom of Jordan rules over a swath of the ancient Fertile Crescent, a valley and rocky area that shared the glory of a richly historical region. The first human activity in the Jordan Valley dates from 10,000 to 6000 B.C.E., from Jericho in the West Bank—the world's oldest continuously inhabited human settlement—to Rama, Wadi Mimrin and Wadi Shu'eib in the East Bank of modern Jordan.[1]

The Cradle of Civilization was taking shape, writes archaeological writer Rami Khouri, as "people were tying themselves down to the soil." The deserts of Syria, Iraq, Egypt, Arabia, and the Sahara were formed around 6000 B.C.E.; huge lakes formed in the heart of what is now Jordan, but dried out and their vicinities emptied of inhabitants, between 4750 and 3750 B.C.E.[2]

Israelites, Ammonites, and Moabites controlled the hills on both sides of the Jordan, until Philistine invaders of 1150 B.C.E. conquered and ruled the valley for 150 years (their name immortalized in the Roman province of Palestine). The Philistines were finally defeated by David, who established the Kingdom of Israel, with Jerusalem as its capital.

Here, almost two thousand years ago, the Nabataeans, a new tribe that moved into southern Jordan from the Arabian Peninsula, carved ingenious water-conserving channels through the majestic red and purple mountains of Petra—a city of dwellings and temples so awesomely chiseled from within stony mountains, and at such imperial height, that it seems inconceivable that mortal man could have accomplished such feats.

Modern Jordan, by contrast, is barely carving out its survival from waters that flow through its earth. The saline lower Jordan is useless, and a lack of carryover storage leads to acute shortages in dry years. Only the underdeveloped stretch of the Yarmuk River carries potential for further exploitation.

"One logical place for Jordan to store water is the Sea of Galilee, because it is both downstream and well defined as a lake to hold water," explained Professor David Eaton, Ben Harris Centennial Professor of Natural Resource Policy Studies at the Lyndon Baines Johnson School of Public Affairs of the University of Texas. "For obvious political and operational reasons, however, Jordan has been unwilling to link its water future to a lake situated within Israel."[3]

More than half of Jordan's de facto annual Yarmuk River share has been "stolen" by Syria. Jordan has consented to Syrian overwithdrawals, but only after severe political pressure from the Syrian government.

In May 1990, Jordan's King Hussein reportedly stated that the one issue that "could bring Jordan to war again is water." The Jordanian government later denied the remark; indeed, water relations between Jordan and Israel have been more like those of contesting allies than of warring adversaries. Water sharing between Israel and Jordan remained relatively stable even during the 1967 and 1973 wars. Israeli authorities therefore dismissed Hussein's alleged statement as a ploy to open up the pipeline of desperately needed Arab aid.

Hussein's wrath, however, may have been directed less at water sharing than at Israeli refusal to concur in World Bank funding for the Wahda ("Unity") Dam on the upper Yarmuk River. The dam would have ensured sorely needed water relief for the Jordan Valley both by providing water storage and by regulating the water supply.

To be situated at the Maqarin site along the Yarmuk between Jordan and Syria, the proposed dam could, in principle, regulate the flow of the Yarmuk by creating storage capacity of 220 million cubic meters per year; minimize the discharge of scarce waters to the Dead Sea; expand irrigated agriculture in the Jordan valley; and provide water for municipal and industrial use in upland Jordan. But the World Bank, by charter, cannot proceed with financial support unless all riparian nations affected by a particular project give their agreement. Israel withheld its approval, contingent on being assured of what it deemed a fair share of Yarmuk waters.

Under the terms of the historic Israel-Jordan peace treaty of October 26, 1994, however, Israel agreed to help Jordan facilitate an upstream dam on the Yarmuk. This cleared the way for international funding. The question is: Will Syrian approval be required for such a dam, and will it be forthcoming?

Survival

Of the Middle East river basins—the Nile, the Tigris-Euphrates, and the Jordan—the Jordan Basin confronts the most acute near-term water shortages.

The most far-reaching plan for Jordan Basin–wide development was achieved in 1953 by Eric Johnston, President Dwight D. Eisenhower's special envoy to the Middle East. The Eisenhower administration had offered its good offices in the dual hope of assisting Arab refugees and helping Israel stand on its feet by rational distribution of Jordan waters. Although technical understandings were reached, and the parties still operate tacitly under many of the provisions discussed, formal acceptance was never achieved.

Nevertheless, the scheme has since served as the basis of American aid to Jordan and Israel for development of their water systems.

The Jordan River is fed by tributaries flowing from Syria and Lebanon into the Sea of Galilee, and from there southward to the Dead Sea. The Yarmuk, the Jordan's primary tributary, ambles forty kilometers between Syria and Jordan before emptying into the Jordan River ten kilometers below the Sea of Galilee.

The Dan, nurtured by springs at its source, is the only stream within the basin that rests entirely within pre-1967 Israel. Its rushing waters surge suddenly into a motionless pool, and then slowly twist into a meandering stream that inches through a densely wooded area of trees thousands of years old. Low arching branches beckon the visitor to their haven of silence. Listen closely and you may even hear a faint whisper from the Garden of Eden.[4]

The Hasbani has its sources in Lebanon, while the Banias —its cascading waterfalls protected by the Greek god Pan— is nurtured primarily by a Syrian spring. Winter rain contributes 50 percent of the river's flow; the remainder comes from springs around the Sea of Galilee.

The Jordan River meets 50 percent of both Israeli and Jordanian water demand. The nation of Jordan, dependent on the Yarmuk tributary for its share, has only been able to use a portion of its Johnston allocation, in part because there has been no available storage capacity until now on the upper Yarmuk.

Jordan devotes most of its meager 20-percent share of Yarmuk waters to agriculture in the Jordan Valley. Yarmuk waters are also pumped through pipelines to upland urban centers, such as Irbid and Amman, for municipal and industrial use.

While Jordan used 871 million cubic meters of Yarmuk waters in 1990, the country's fully developed resources have a renewal capacity of only 635 million cubic meters per year. Jordan met the 236-million-cubic-meter deficit in 1990, and since, by overdrawing on groundwater basins in excess of their sustainable yield, and by pumping from the fossil aquifer in Disi.

The kingdom is looking longingly at the Yarmuk for an additional 350 million cubic meters per year, a sum that could increase renewable resources by as much as 40 percent. Jordan has long claimed that Syria is taking twice its Johnston-apportioned share from the Yarmuk, and that Israel is also taking more than its share.

Syria has already built over thirty medium and small dams, with more underway, that could eventually divert up to 40 percent of the Yarmuk waters if terms of agreement with Jordan are not observed. Absent Jordanian agreement, Syria's dam scheme will simply take longer to complete (perhaps another decade), and will sharpen the rivalry between the two nations in the interim. Syria's further diversion of the Yarmuk would mean a drastic loss for Jordan, which even the water benefits of the peace with Israel could not replace.

Jordan's Empty Aquifers

A significant proportion of both Israel's and Jordan's population is concentrated in the Jordan Basin, while Syria's basin population is centered around the Yarmuk and the Sea of Galilee region. High-quality basin soils have been extensively developed by all riparians. Jordan uses approximately 130 million cubic meters of the annual

Yarmuk flow for irrigated agriculture. Its agriculturally based economy produces wheat, barley, lentils, fruit, olives, vegetables, and tobacco, while Israel concentrates on citrus, melons, bananas, tomatoes, groundnuts, celery, avocados, flowers, and cotton.

Jordan's population, like Syria's, is growing at an explosive rate. The official Jordanian rate is 4 percent, but officials insist that waves of Palestinian refugees push the figure closer to 8 percent (an additional three hundred thousand refugees arrived in Jordan during and after the Gulf War crisis).

Jordan's two-hundred-cubic-meter per capita share of freshwater resources in 1992 was less than 10 percent of the 1948 figure. A country is typically considered water-short when per capita share is one thousand cubic meters per year.

Renewable water sources, as well as limited quantities of nonrenewable fossil groundwater, are available in southern Jordan, but at a distance of three hundred kilometers from the major city centers. Nonrenewable resources could vanish in fifty years, if drawn at the present rate of 140 million cubic meters per year.

Jordan's aquifers have been progressively depleted, resulting in lower water quality and yield. Deep aquifer potentials have not yet been examined. The water in such aquifers is presumed to be of marginal quality, and the cost of drilling is prohibitively high.

The nation's main aquifer, the Qa-disi, has 50 percent less water than originally calculated, and its waters must be transported 350 kilometers to heavy population areas. The Al Azaraq Oasis springs, north of Amman, are almost completely dry. Aquifers shared with Syria (the Azraq, Amman-Zarqa, Yarmuk, and Hammad), with Saudi Arabia (the Hamad, Sirhan-Hammad, and Disi), and with Iraq (the Hamad), are a fundamental concern. Unilateral development by Jordan's neighbors would disastrously affect Jordan's future.

Jordan has made vast strides in irrigation and municipal and industrial water services, but its agricultural base is more limited than in many arid countries. Only 50 percent of rain-fed areas are cultivated, and they produce only 22 percent of the nation's total food requirements. Irrigated agriculture supplies 16 percent of the food consumed. By 2010, Jordan will need 8 billion cubic meters of water to achieve a food trade balance.

To meet a 45-percent deficit in waters for Jordan Valley agriculture in 1991, Jordan drew upon 170 percent of its renewable groundwater resources. Upland irrigation waters were supplied in part by using and depleting renewable and fossil groundwater.

Nevertheless, combined municipal and industrial demand will claim nearly 75 percent of the country's total renewable waters by 2010. As in Israel, wastewater could provide a key portion of the country's renewable resources, but this would require expensive treatment technology and costly environmental safeguards.

In the summer of 1991, Amman received only 48 hours of water per week; in the summer of 1994, Israeli Prime Minister Yitzhak Rabin ordered the immediate transfer to Jordan of 4 million cubic meters of Yarmuk waters to relieve acute drinking water shortages in Amman and Irbid. "This is a gesture of goodwill," Jordan's peace negotiator, Fayez al-Tarawneh, declared in a Reuter's interview.

The gift of water followed the historic signing of the Washington Declaration by Prime Minister Rabin and King Hussein of Jordan on July 25, 1994. The declaration ended a 46-year state of belligerency between Jordan and Israel. But Israel, on its own, cannot relieve Jordan's water stress. International action and financial support for Jordan's water dilemmas are the paramount priority.

"I come before you today fully conscious of the need to secure a peace for all the children of Abraham," King Hussein stated in his riveting address before the U.S. Congress on July 26, 1994. One hopes that the Jordanian child will not again be forgotten by the world in the rush of future events.

10

THE WATER SUMMIT THAT WASN'T

Water is an issue of life and death for Syria.
But if it is a choice between defending
ourselves against our enemy, Israel, or turning
our attention to this matter, we will choose
to accept death for our people.

—former Syrian diplomat

Significant insights can often be gleaned more from plans gone awry than from those that actually succeed. The Middle East water summit, to be held November 4 through 9, 1991—the first regional meeting planned between Israel and her Arab neighbors on the vital issue of water, and the fruit of years of preparation—did not take place.

But as the Shoemaker-Levy Comet, in its collision with Jupiter, revealed much about that planet's atmosphere, so the failed summit left a trail of light that richly illuminates the shadowy substance and tangled terrain of Middle East water politics.

Hosted by then-president of Turkey Turgut Ozal, and convened by this writer with the Turkish Foreign Ministry, the summit was canceled on October 1, 1991, a month before high-level guests were to arrive in Istanbul. Almost two-thirds of the Arab states had accepted the invitation, including Jordan and Egypt.

President Ozal, who died in 1993, had secretly dreamed of leaving a water legacy. Above all, he wanted to be remembered as the visionary who forged water dialogue over regional gullies and fords. Instead, this political "fox" was cast into the role of quarry by regional nuances and American policies he couldn't seem to grasp—and by his own fears.

Unknown to Turgut Ozal, as well as to summit conveners at the time, was the fact that the water summit endangered the closely guarded secret of the senior U.S. State Department officials in charge of the peace process: that Syria had no intention of participating in multilateral talks associated with the Madrid Peace Conference, and least of all in direct discussions with Israel on water. On the very day that the Middle East water summit was canceled, Syrian Foreign Minister Farouq Al-Schara told a reporter, "Israel has no right even to a single drop of water in this region."

Moreover, the same American players allegedly concluded that if Israel were allowed to attend a multilateral dialogue with Arab states outside of the formal peace framework, critical U.S. leverage would be lost over the Likud-led Israeli government.

And when the final curtain fell on this water saga, it was another man, one high on America's "blacklist" at the time (during and in the aftermath of the Gulf War), who emerged as the lone combattant for a regional approach to water peace: Crown Prince Hassan of Jordan. (Jordan is a geographically small country with a long border with Iraq. Desperately seeking to remain neutral during Operation Storm, the country paid a high price in official U.S. rage.) Even with the heralded Madrid Peace Conference taking shape, the failed water conference was characterized by Crown Prince Hassan in August 1991 as "another nail in the coffin of the Middle East." While recent political breakthroughs suggest a more optimistic picture, only time —and future water developments—can divine the measure of truth in this assessment.

Opening Curtain

What follows, then, is the tale of a real-life episode that felt more like a movie for those caught in the drama.

The 1991 summit had its roots in a secret 1987 conference on the region's water future, convened by this writer under the sponsorship of the Center for Strategic and International Studies in Washington, D.C. The governments of Israel, Jordan, Iraq, Turkey, and Egypt boldly sent high-level representatives to a dialogue that continued unabated for three days.

The historic magnitude of these discussions suggested the value of even larger and more creative steps toward Middle East water discussions. Thus a nongovernmental organization, the Global Water Summit Initiative (GWSI), was founded by this writer in January 1989 with the primary goal of convening a Middle East water summit.

This writer first met Turgut Ozal in 1984, when his personality still resonated with the enthusiasm and energy of the victorious underdog in the race for his nation's highest public office—he had been elected prime minister less than a year earlier, in November 1983. He greeted his guest in shirtsleeves, laughed and jested, and transmitted boundless excitement for the cause of Turkey.

An Iraqi guide once told me of the time he accompanied Turgut Ozal to an archaeological site in sweltering 120-degree midday sun. This guide, along with his Iraqi colleagues, was overcome by the heat and soon ran to his car for shelter; but Ozal, a stocky man who would later develop serious heart trouble, strode purposefully forward with nary a trace of fatigue.

In 1989, Turkey was the only Middle East nation aside from Egypt that had diplomatic ties with both Israel and Arab nations. Given the country's then-growing reputation as a bridge to the West, its abundant water supplies, and an innovative prime minister with whom I had established a professional relationship, it seemed natural that Turgut Ozal should be asked to serve as summit host.

Boutros Boutros-Ghali, the first regional leader approached on this matter in early 1989, chose to stress the African, rather than Middle Eastern, dimension of Egypt's water role. The African Water Summit, which this writer co-convened with Boutros-Ghali in 1990, became both a precursor and a profound learning experience for organizers of the 1991 Middle East event.

Counter Conditions: The Israeli Invitation

I presented Turgut Ozal with only one condition: that no Middle Eastern country could be excluded from this water conference, specifically not the state of Israel. With a crumpled copy of my letter in hand, Ozal responded in a March 1989 meeting, "This is a good thing; we shall do it."

He in turn presented an even more imposing condition. Israel would be invited, but only *if* the United Nations and the World Bank were convinced to provide an umbrella of international sponsorship for the conference. (Ozal, a World Bank officer in his younger years, was searching for new inroads to this august financial establishment.)

Although it was a daunting request, Ozal's demands were nevertheless met by the fall of 1990. After a seemingly endless round of meetings and letters, the World Bank, the United Nations Development Programme (UNDP), and the United Nations Environment Programme (UNEP) finally agreed to help sponsor the effort.

The summit goal: to create a regional dialogue on water management and a common framework for water security. A triangular strategy was adopted, involving top-level Mideast decision-makers, donor funds and institutions, and the private sector. The substantive process was to be reinforced by the creation of a broad financial mechanism for donor and private-sector participation: the Middle East Water Trust.

At the summit, senior officers from regionally based development finance institutions were to discuss failures and successes of past and ongoing water projects; funding for future feasibility studies; co-financing arrangements; and the pooling of technical assistance among the fifteen major development funds currently existing in the region for the identification and support of water-related infrastructure projects.

Conference participants included heads of state, ministers, directors general of the various ministries, heads of water authorities, and government experts. The summit agenda was divided into three days of preparatory technical forums, followed by two days of ministerial dialogue.

The agenda also involved discussion of a "regional water community" or body, similar to the European Coal and Steel Community created by the Marshall Plan following World War II. Its suggested functions would include coordination of parallel water planning among all Middle East nations, regional data collection, cooperative research, emergency response mechanisms, dispute resolution, and the setting up of a water and environmental "peace corps" for children in the region.

Communications were undertaken with decision-makers throughout the region and around the world to convey the critical dimensions of the Mideast water problem and the urgent need for a creative international response.

After lengthy negotiations undertaken by this writer, senior World Bank officials agreed to send a team of experts to twenty-two regional countries, including Israel, to help encourage and coordinate the delivery of country papers at the conference. UNDP participation was viewed as a special achievement, as this is the largest implementing agency for global water projects.

Thus empowered, Turgut Ozal (who was elected president of Turkey in November 1989) proceeded at the end of November 1990 to send personal invitations to the heads of state of Middle East nations, to Presidents George Bush and Mikhail Gorbachev, to the leaders of all Western nations, and also to India, China, and other key nonaligned countries that were invited to participate as observers. This was to be a grand meeting, indeed.

Much to the shock of the organizers, however, it was

quickly discovered that the state of Israel had been excluded from the president's lengthy list. With the conference almost a year away and Iraq's invasion of Kuwait raising war drums in the region, Ozal had decided that Turkey should wait before raising an Israeli "red flag" in Istanbul.

The Letter on Ice

The plot now begins to take shape: The Bush White House had induced President Turgut Ozal to step forward boldly as a key U.S. player in the Gulf War alliance. The Republic of Turkey, from the time of its founding in 1920, had previously adhered to a policy of strict regional neutrality. In crossing this divide, Ozal understood that he could jeopardize crucial domestic support in forthcoming elections planned for October 1991. (Indeed, the Motherland Party's loss in these elections was due in no small part to Ozal's Gulf War actions on behalf of the United States.)

Yet Ozal's letter to the president of the United States concerning the Istanbul water summit never reached the White House. This missive, it was later learned, was initially shunted through various bureaus of the Department of State, and later, rather remarkably, to an assistant secretary of the Department of the Interior who bore no particular responsibility for Middle East issues. Having received no instructions for reply, he simply "put it in my safe and forgot about it."

Ozal had assumed from the outset that he enjoyed the goodwill of the U.S. administration. Turkey, after all, was a key U.S. ally. Moreover, U.S. agencies had helped fund the

1990 African Water Summit in Cairo, with accolades for the organizers. The glove was a perfect fit, and expectations ran high.

In March 1991, the Department of State assented to a briefing by the summit organizers. Seated around an oblong conference table, fifteen officials listened to a description by this writer of the rationale behind the planned event, and a litany of accomplishments. The summit, they were told, was not an end point, but the launching pad for a long-term regional strategy that would engage all levels of society from the top echelons to the technical and corporate, as well as the grass roots.

Crown Prince Hassan of Jordan and Boutros Boutros-Ghali of Egypt, they were informed, would be giving keynote addresses, as would Maurice Strong, leader of the United Nations Earth Summit in Rio. The World Bank and relevant UN agencies were engaged, and one of the largest Arab development funds would join as a sponsor. There was reason to hope that the head of the Gulf Cooperation Council might address the summit (a commitment which was confirmed in early August 1991). Ozal's promise to issue an invitation to Israel was recounted, and the organizers expressed hope that the U.S. government would actively assist the Turkish leader in overcoming potential Arab resistance.

The Pipeline Minefield

Ozal had earlier assured the conveners that Israel's invitation would be extended no later than the first week of August. But suddenly there was an imposing glitch in the timing. Syria had advised Turkish officials in mid-June that if Israel was invited, Syria would not only refuse to participate, but would launch a campaign to keep all other Arab nations from attending as well.

Secretly, however, there was another and equally significant cause for Syrian concern. Much to the chagrin of Syrians, let alone the organizers, Ozal had been assiduously trying to link the conference with his dream for the establishment of a $20 billion Peace Water Pipeline that would carry water from Turkey to water-starved countries throughout the Middle East, traversing both Syria and Saudi Arabia. On the surface, the pipeline carried the aura of a benevolent and sorely needed solution to the region's acute water problems. The Syrians, however, viewed the pipeline as final proof of perfidious Turkish intentions to restore the power of the Ottoman Empire. A high Syrian official explained to a World Bank representative visiting Damascus in June 1991, "We have already told Mr. Ozal that we reject the peace pipeline; if the summit is going to be the peace pipeline, we are not interested, and we are not going." The Syrian minister of foreign affairs and his legal adviser made it clear in a three-hour meeting with this World Bank consultant that "we are doing very well with the Turks in the negotiations on the Euphrates. If the conference addresses the peace pipeline, it will hurt our progress."

The water-poor Saudi government was meanwhile letting it be known that even if a Turkish water pipeline could provide a sorely needed drinking water supply, it wanted no part of a project that would give Turkey the remotest option (and leverage) of controlling the tap.

Refusing to acknowledge Syrian, Saudi, and wider regional fears of Turkish aspirations for regional water dominance—by now broadly shared in coded diplomatic tones

—Ozal persisted in trumpeting the pipeline at the loudest possible decibel level. But he was head cheerleader of a squad of relatively few champions.

Apart from a subtle duel of influence being waged over future engineering contracts in the area, notably among major U.S. contractors and the U.S. Army Corps of Engineers, even leading Turkish political figures were adamantly opposed to the plan.

This included then–former president Süleyman Demirel, and also Foreign Minister Sefa Giray, both of whom contended that in ten years' time, Turkey would not have enough water for its own populace. "We will have 70 million people by the year 2000," Giray told this writer, "and we will not have enough water for our own people."

Summit organizers found themselves in an eye-of-a-tiger dilemma: How to calm Syrian fears about Ozal's pipeline concept—which was not even on the official conference agenda—while convincing Ozal that Syrian threats about boycotting in the event of Israeli participation could, at least in part, be interpreted as a smokescreen?

Is Too Late Better Than Never?

However, even if Turgut Ozal had been moved in mid-July to consider Syrian sensibilities, it was already too late.

According to information provided by sources close to Hafiz al-Assad, the president of Syria raised his opposition to Israel's participation in meetings with senior U.S. officials the second week of July. Assad was reportedly told by his American visitors: "This conference is not important; you do not have to attend it."

Thereafter, it was irrelevant whether Ozal aggravated or

placated his Syrian counterparts—though no one involved with the summit understood it at the time. The U.S. government had effectively quashed the event.

In his meeting with President Bush in July 1991, President Ozal raised the question of the Istanbul conference and the Israeli invitation, expressing his hope for administration support. Bush, according to Turkish officials, remained silent. "The President was fully briefed," stated a former American diplomat. "He simply played dumb." Ozal, unfortunately, misread this nonresponse as an affirmation.

Turkey's prime minister, Yildirim Akbulut, also mentioned the water event to President Bush, stating categorically that Israel would be invited; Foreign Minister Sefa Giray, favoring the invitation, instructed ministry officials to prepare the groundwork.

As Secretary of State James Baker's Mideast peace "shuttle" moved into full throttle, the U.S. Department of the Interior official, who had Ozal's letter to President Bush in his wall safe, suddenly received a call from a member of the National Security Council directing him to draft and sign a noncommittal response to Ozal's invitation.

"I told him I have no authority to commit the president, that frankly, I didn't know how to answer the letter, and that I couldn't answer the letter. It was the most peculiar thing I have ever seen," commented the Interior Department official.

When organizers further requested that U.S. embassy officials based in Arab countries be given a green light by the administration to mention the water conference in a positive context, they were told: "We cannot interfere with a private effort." Thereafter, only limited communication was tendered by the U.S. government—primarily in the form of late-summer suggestions that the summit be canceled.

Sources of funding pledged earlier in the year by three government agencies (none in the foreign policy field) dried up faster than rainwater in the desert. The water conference, it appeared, had been derailed at a very high level. One lower-ranking official in a trade-related agency even received a "Deep Throat"–style call noting that his job could be on the line if he recommended that his agency provide support.

The purported reason for the opposition of the State Department's peace-negotiating team was the absence of an Israeli invitation. In reality, the water summit was now viewed as a noise factor that should be eliminated at the earliest possible date.

Turgut Ozal, master politician, was still unable to fathom the political writing on the wall. He stubbornly clung to the conviction that George Bush would rally to his side and use American "chits" to persuade Assad to drop his objections to, or at least his campaign against, Israeli participation.

While Ozal's initial letter to President Bush remained unanswered, he nevertheless decided on August 8, 1991, to write once again. This time he stressed the need for immediate assistance on the Syrian front. The man who had challenged the entrenched political party structure of Turkey in 1984, and won, feared that if he went out on a limb against Syria in 1991, he would lose.

"Dear Mr. President," wrote Ozal, according to details provided by his closest aides, "I am writing you to request your full support for the Middle East water summit. . . . I understand the importance of Israel's participation, and I wish to invite the state of Israel. This is my intention. I have not been able to extend the invitation until now because of Syrian and other Arab opposition. I need your help." He further asked that official U.S. opposition to the summit be lifted.

A series of ironic twists soon followed. One pro-Israel group put out the word that the entire controversy should really be blamed on Saudi Arabia, since attacks against Syria could hurt administration strategies for the peace process. A pro-Palestinian group, by contrast, forwarded a letter to the U.S. Secretary of State requesting his support in convincing Syria to allow Israel to attend the conference.

A well-placed Syrian diplomat, highly sensitive to his country's critical water future, launched a last-ditch effort to find a compromise solution. ("When the school bell rings in the afternoon," the Syrian pointed out, "you see nothing but children for miles and miles; but how will we feed all of these children?") He suggested to Damascus that the Istanbul meeting be reconstituted as a low-level international technical forum, without ministerial representation, thus enabling Syria to attend—but he never received a reply.

At almost the same juncture, a key official in the Israeli prime minister's office concluded that there was at least as much to be gained from exposing Syrian intransigence on the water summit as from actually participating in the conference. Having been quietly alerted to Ozal's latest letter gambit, this official leaked the news to the vociferous Israeli press. Thus, by the time Ozal's letter reached the White House, a flurry of press rumors was hovering over Washington, D.C.

Ozal's second epistle had no better fate than the first. By early September 1991, American officials were insisting that the region's water problems would be quickly dealt with once the Madrid Peace Conference was convened. The statements of lower-level aides, however, were more revealing.

"Frankly, we're grasping at a wet cake of soap that keeps shooting off in all directions," admitted a State Department deputy assistant secretary in September 1991. "The water idea is out there, but it's fuzzily defined. The way that the top level looks at the problem, practical economic aspects are subsumed under political issues. You could say that we're dealing in a murky environment."

The Madrid Peace Conference took place in October 1991, with great fanfare and hope. It was announced that multilateral working forums on water, the environment, economic cooperation, arms control, and refugee resettlement were being organized—which was indeed the case. A former U.S. ambassador, intimately aware of Bush administration thinking on the multilateral forums, insisted in a public debate, "The beauty of the approach is that there is no single vision that can lock us into a failure."

Turkish offers to play a prominent role in the Madrid peace process by hosting the opening multilateral forum (on virtually any topic) were met with silence. (As of September 1994, Turkey still had not been invited to host a multilateral forum.) Incredulity on the Turkish side that their president could be treated in such a manner bespoke Turkish assumptions about government-to-government relations with the United States. Ozal and his closest aides could not accept even the notion that he might have been purposefully undercut. "We know that these actions are really caused by the Jewish lobby," a senior aide confided.

Should President Turgut Ozal have been accorded greater respect and support from the U.S. government? Could Syrian resistance have been overcome or at least modified? Should the Istanbul water summit have been permitted to take place, if at a later date? The summit's demise left more questions than answers.

Sources suggest that Crown Prince Hassan of Jordan, alone among world leaders, quietly attempted to persuade the Syrian government to let the summit go forward as planned.

History should at least record his intervention.

11 THE REPUBLIC OF TURKEY: *Space Odyssey 2001*

A republic is a raft which will never sink,
but our feet are always in the water.
—Fisher Ames,
Speech in the House
of Representatives, 1795

Nine months after the summit's collapse, the Foreign Ministry of Turkey tracked me down in Israel to request that I be their guest at the opening ceremony of the Ataturk Dam on July 24, 1992. They were insistent, phoning at least ten times during the course of a week for final arrangements. The trip itself would prove at least as instructive about the Turkish mentality as about Turkish approaches to water security.

I had hardly imagined that I would be returning to Turkey almost a year after President Turgut Ozal made his fateful decision to cancel the Middle East water summit. Yet a year later, the flag of Israel was flying from President Ozal's car, honoring the first visit of an Israeli president to the Republic of Turkey. President Chaim Herzog was attending the five-hundred-year celebration of the Jewish presence in Turkey.

I was personally reluctant to return to reminders of an extremely painful experience, but at the same time professionally intrigued by the insistent manner of the approach. What was on their minds?

I departed for Istanbul on July 23. The plane was delayed by three hours, which meant an eleven P.M. arrival. The Foreign Ministry official who was to meet me had been told that the plane wasn't arriving until midnight. I found myself outside the Istanbul airport, with no escort, no Turkish money, and no hotel.

At that point I asked a man walking by if he spoke English. Indeed he did, and was also one of the kindest strangers you could hope to meet in such a situation. Mr. Aya and his wife drove me to a nearby hotel, spent an hour trying to reach the Foreign Ministry official by phone, and invited me to their home for dinner the next evening. By extraordinary coincidence, Mr. Aya was in charge of a key component of the Ataturk Dam project.

Turkish officials insisted with apologies that a car would be provided to take me to Prime Minister Demirel's press conference the following morning. It never arrived. The explanation: "We forgot." Arriving by taxi, I was greeted by a hundred or so policemen, many training their guns in my direction. I spent an hour in fruitless pleading before a Turkish reporter took pity and cleared the diplomatic hurdles that would gain me entry.

Demirel was underscoring the critical importance of democracy when I entered the room. Built like a football player, he had the tolerant look of an aging coach, rather than the look of a seven-time prime minister who had also spent time in prison at the hands of the military.

Dr. Sule Kut, a leading female academic, explained that

Turkey's democratic constitution is on a par with those of the most developed nations of the world. She spoke about the incredible advancement of women in Turkey over the last decade—there were more female Turkish doctors proportionately than in the United States (and in 1993 there would be a female prime minister, Tansu Ciller)—and the longing of the Turkish people for a secular, developed nation.

After the luncheon buffet, I and about thirty other members of the press went directly to a waiting plane. Here we were in Turkey, flying Moldava Airlines, with a Russian pilot. It seems the Turkish charter company had bought a bunch of old Russian Republic planes on the cheap, including their pilots.

Most of the seats were broken, floorboards were coming loose, and the bathroom looked like it hadn't recovered from the Second World War. "That's not my problem," said the stewardess.

A sometimes air-conditioned bus drove us three and a half hours to a midnight dinner served literally on the ground, per local custom, and hosted by the area governor. The governor had gone to sleep, but the food was delicious. We sat in lotus positions, or the equivalent, happily taking in the food, the yogurt drink, and the brilliant stars in one chorus. Early the following morning we began an additional hour and a half's journey to the Ataturk Dam ceremony.

Restoring Turkey's Place in History

Six hours of driving had still produced little sign of civilization, short of the miniature town where we had stayed overnight. The countryside was desertlike, barren of homes or people, but by no means a desert. Grass and weeds were struggling to survive, where the people had given up long ago. Half of the original population of the southeastern Anatolia area, or six hundred thousand people, had emigrated to the greater Istanbul area over the last decade. A sizable Kurdish population still resides in the area. The megacity of Istanbul, by contrast, is packed with 20 million people, or 40 percent of Turkey's population. Traffic is so bottlenecked there that it makes the streets of Cairo look like a superhighway. Convincing Istanbul citizens to relocate to the southeastern Anatolia area is deemed a vital national priority.

Specialists in water politics typically analyze the South East Anatolia Development Project (GAP) and the damming of the Euphrates in terms of Turkey's relations with Syria and Iraq. From the perspective of the bus window, however, one began to understand that the goal is nothing short of national survival.

Generously endowed with water, Turkey controls the headwaters of the Tigris and Euphrates rivers. Yet 40 percent of Turkey's arable land is in southeastern Anatolia, where there is a general shortage of water. To alleviate this shortage, Turkey initiated the GAP project in 1983. GAP is made up of a series of thirteen irrigation and hydroelectric dam sites, including the massive Ataturk Dam. Seven of these sites are located on the Euphrates River, and the other six are on the Tigris.

Upon completion, the project will supply approximately 24 billion kilowatt-hours of energy (almost half of Turkey's current energy needs), and open 1.6 million hectares of land to irrigated cultivation. The Turkish government hopes to sell the additional food production to Europe and the Middle East, which is expected to import $20 billion worth of foodstuffs by the end of the century.

Arrival at the Ataturk Dam, the largest in the thirteen-dam network, is a shock, to be sure. The Ataturk is the ninth-largest dam on the globe, but in its context, could easily be counted as one of the wonders of the world.

Shuttle to the Next Century

There, in the middle of nowhere, with the heat reaching over 120 degrees in the shade, is a resplendent feat of space-age engineering, which was completely financed, designed, and built by the Turkish government and Turkish companies.

"The experts laughed at us," the head of the consortium that built the project told the audience. "They invited us to a special conference on dams in Los Angeles to prove that it couldn't be done, especially not by Turkish contractors. But we completed the construction in record speed."

Then–prime minister Turgut Ozal, who approved the initial $100 million grant, had instructed the team, "You will finish rapidly and the Ataturk Dam will be the pride of Turkey." The dam was completed two to three years ahead of schedule because of his support.

Two tunnels, each with a diameter of 7.62 meters and a length of 26.4 kilometers, have been constructed underneath mountains to carry water to the outlying areas. The land to be irrigated by the Sanhurfa water tunnels, the most fertile part of the region, was known centuries ago as Upper Mesopotamia.

Critics say the money poured into the project fueled inflation, and that it will be ten to twenty years before the returns are felt by the population. But in this time period, Turkey will have established the largest citrus plant in the world, increased vegetable production by 40 percent, and the production of cows by 50 percent. By 2015, Turkey will have the potential to serve as the breadbasket of the Middle East, as well as parts of Europe.

Turkish decision-makers understand the need for food security better than most, and are adamantly determined to ensure an ample supply for future generations. "We do not tell the Arabs how to use their oil," noted Demirel. "They cannot tell us how to use our water."

Demirel, an engineer by training and first director of the state water planning authority, laid the foundation for GAP as prime minister in 1965. "Prime Minister Demirel knows more about dams than the combined knowledge of all of the contractors who worked on this project," declared the director of the ATA consortium, which constructed the dam.

Over a thousand notables had arrived that day from all over Turkey, as well as presidents and prime ministers from many other countries. Each VIP was handed his own GAP umbrella for the scorching walk to the tent-covered stands. The punishing noon hour was tied to the filing needs of the press—an indication of the extent to which Turkish officials were prepared to suffer to get headline coverage in the morning papers.

"We have started down the path of a great tomorrow," Demirel stated in his official remarks. "Turkey is great and it will be greater. Turkey is unified and it will remain unified. Everything will be more beautiful. The main thing is to support one another and to have faith in one another. I congratulate you, and God bless you."

Wilting guests rallied to his remarks with thunderous

applause, including the former general who had sentenced Demirel to prison and was now seated in the same front row.

President Ozal, an ardent political foe of Demirel, recalled the tenth anniversary of the founding of the Turkish republic, "when we sang with all of our might about how we built railways from all corners of Turkey. We were taught to trust ourselves and to make a positive contribution," he said. "When I was sent to study in the United States I was shocked by what the Americans had accomplished," Ozal noted. "But our aim has been to make Turkey the biggest and most important state."

Between 1923 and 1950, 3 dams were built in Turkey; 6 were built in the 1950s. There are now 140 dams, but no other is equal to the raw power of the Ataturk Dam. "The twenty-first century will be our era," Ozal shouted triumphantly, as he executed the protocol honor of pushing the button that started the generators. At precisely that moment, firecrackers lit the sky, hand gliders circled the dam, balloons were flying, and the music from *2001: A Space Odyssey* resonated from every corner of the dam and bleachers.

The choice of music spoke of the pride of a nation. Basic coordination of transportation may still be a challenge, but for the Republic of Turkey, the Ataturk Dam is a space shuttle to the next century.

Turkey Is Not the Middle East Water Savior

Despite the flurry of press over the last several years—and statements of any number of academics—touting Turkey as the potential water savior for the entire Middle East, the leadership is duly concerned that its present water surplus could vanish in thirty years with the accelerated agriculture, tourism, and urbanization expected from the GAP project.

Turkey's water wealth is not unlimited. Annual rainfall of 643 million cubic meters is not evenly distributed over time and place; usable flow in twenty-six drainage basins is hindered by seasonal variation and limited storage capacity. Usable surface flows, combined with exploitable groundwater and inflow from other countries, provide Turkey with only 110 billion cubic meters of exploitable water. Demand, presently at 53 billion cubic meters, will be 74 billion by the year 2000.

Turkey is oil-poor and thus a highly energy-importing nation (it paid $3.5 billion for imported crude oil in 1990). Future substitution of hydropower for thermal power will save Turkey substantial and much-needed foreign currency. The development of hydropower to expand Turkey's industrial base and create employment is a national priority no less urgent than agricultural goals. The Tigris and Euphrates rivers account for one-third of Turkey's hydropotential.

"No Turkish politician in his right mind will suggest giving water away or selling it to anybody else as long as the taps are dry in Turkish cities," said water expert John Kolars, referring to severe water shortages in the larger cities of western Turkey. While Turkish leaders have indeed publicly offered to sell Turkey's waters—notably in President Ozal's much-touted dream of a Turkish peace pipeline, and Prime Minister Tansu Ciller's August 1994 proposal to sell limited water to Israel by tanker—no concrete steps have yet been taken toward fulfillment of these offers.

One can also imagine that the specter of thirsting hordes of Islamic peoples from the Central Asian republics descending on Turkey must be an omnipresent government nightmare. In some parts of the Islamic Aral Sea region, pollution from the sea and poisons from the local water-dependent cotton economy have contaminated all available drinking water. Women in the area are advised against nursing their children because their own milk is toxic. In Central Asia, 90 percent of all hospitals lack sewage facilities, 65 percent are without hot water, and 20 percent lack all running water; 80 percent of all young children in these republics suffer from serious illnesses. "The largest industry in our area is emigration," moaned a weary official. Turkey is a singularly attractive destination.

12

SYRIA'S PERIL, LEBANON'S PLENTY

The conscious water saw its God, and blushed.
—Richard Crashaw,
Epigrammata Sacra, 1634

Sitting in the lobby of the Damascus Sheraton hotel some years ago, lulled by the sound of Muzak emanating from the ceiling, I found myself listening to Israel's nation anthem, "Hatikva"!

I just about collapsed in my chair, then looked discreetly about the room to scc if anyone else had noticed. No one had. (Is this a test, I thought, a wry joke, or just an accident?)

Syria is a nation of contradictions. Damascus, for example, has the potential to be one of the most beautiful cities in the world, with wide boulevards, a colorful mix of baroque and Islamic architecture, and the mystique of an ancient culture still very much in evidence. At the same time, dreary, boxlike socialist structures destroy the view. Foreign visitors are watched, and more than occasionally followed. People speak in whispered tones if the subject is politically suggestive, or refuse to speak at all; too often one hears that a person's relatives or friends are languishing in political prison.

The Syrian people, it must be noted, hunger for news of life in the United States, and were graciously hospitable to this American during the very week in 1981 when U.S. and Syrian forces were shelling each other in Lebanon.

The Syrian countryside is occasionally magnificent, but mostly mountainous and dry. The narrow coastal belt, which benefits from abundant rain, accounts for 88 percent of the country's farming area. Inland rainfall is suitable only for dry farming of wheat, barley, and summer crops.

The International Center for Agricultural Research in Dry Areas (ICARDA) maintains a research facility near Aleppo, which, like Israeli counterparts in the Negev, is trying to develop new strains of crops that can withstand the Syrian climate. While Syria claims that its attempts to reclaim agricultural lands have led to an agricultural revolution, the U.S. Department of State's 1993–94 country profile on Syria describes the country's irrigation schemes, particularly those connected with the Euphrates, as a disappointment.[1]

Syria's antiquated irrigation system, which loses over 50 percent of its water before it reaches the crops, is vastly corroded by salts and fertilizers. Government attention has turned instead to rain-fed lands, which still account for 80 percent of the country's cropped area.

Signaling Danger

A cable from the U.S. embassy in Damascus in December 1993, directed rather remarkably to the senior United

States military commander in Europe, reported that water cutbacks to Syrian farmers had dangerously increased concentrations of fecal matter on irrigated fruits and vegetables, leading to an acute rise in gastrointestinal disorders.

Hazardous materials threaten not only the infrastructure, but the lives of the Syrian people. Aleppo residents endured a cholera outbreak in 1989 that was blamed on contaminated parsley. Yet further Syrian outbreaks of cholera, typhoid, and dysentery have been quietly hidden from the Western media.

Daily government-directed cutoffs of water and of water-driven electricity haunt the country, often as many as nine hours a day. Rural demand and industrialization compound the problem. Syria's Omar and Sijan oilfields, for example, require consistent, reliable, and inexpensive water and power. Fighting an uphill water battle, the government devoted almost a quarter of its 1993 budget of $61 billion to the water and power sectors.

The 1991 drought depressed Turkey's economy, but Syria's situation was even worse. The low level of the Euphrates, combined with pollution from Syrian pesticides, chemicals, and salt, forced the government to drastically reduce the supply of both drinking water and electricity to Damascus, Aleppo, and several other cities. Damascus is still without water many nights, and is estimated to lose as much as 30 to 40 percent of its drinking water from old, leaking pipes.

Aleppo's primary water source, the Quwayq River, was reduced to a trickle decades ago when upstream farmers diverted its waters for irrigation. The city's water source is so deep below the ground that there are insufficient funds to tap it, and water is therefore piped all the way from the Euphrates.

Syria is actively seeking international funding for key projects. The Kuwait Fund for Arab Economic Development channeled a $63 million loan to Syria for the Tishreen Dam project; the European Community has pledged $7.5 million for a water supply project in Hama.

The Syrian-Jordanian Great Yarmuk project, if realized, will withdraw 70 million cubic meters per year for irrigation farming in southern Syria, and 700 million for irrigation and hydropower in Jordan. Syria is also building a canal to divert approximately 125 million cubic meters per year from Hasbani Jordan River headwaters.

Food security is deemed an urgent priority in Syria. The Islamic Network on Water Resources determined that 1,295 cubic meters of water per person are required annually to produce an average daily diet of 3,000 to 3,500 calories. Yet Syrian population growth alone will lead in the next twenty-five years to a 50-percent drop in per capita supply.

Turkey's Water Fortune Is Syria's Misery

"The Euphrates is the backbone of our economy" proclaimed Hafiz al-Assad in an interview with the Arabic-language *Tishrin,* in March 1994. "Perhaps it is the significance of this basin that has turned our attention primarily to agricultural development as a means to fulfill the concept of food security."

Syria relies on the Euphrates for more than 80 percent of its waters. Desalination of Mediterranean waters is still a distant, and much too expensive dream, while other unconventional water techniques, such as drip irrigation, are also too costly for wide use.

Under the terms of a 1987 agreement, Turkey guaranteed Syria a minimum of five hundred cubic meters of water per second at the Turkish-Syrian border. In turn, Syria has been diverting 52 percent of the flow to Iraq.

Syria fears, however, that the Ataturk Dam will divert between 30 to 50 percent of the Euphrates' flow into Turkey's Urfa Plain, forcing Syria as well as Iraq into the role of hydrological dependents. Syria's Tabqa Dam has been affected. "Only two of the dam's eight turbines are working," said a senior official to *National Geographic*'s Priit Vasiland. "There has never been enough water for them all."

Turkey alarmed her downstream co-riparians in early November 1989, by announcing that it would hold back the flow of the Euphrates for one month, starting in January 1990, in order to begin filling the Ataturk dam. Some Middle East sources have suggested that Saddam Hussein read this action as part of a U.S. plot against Iraq.

To allay concerns, the Turkish government provided "detailed technical information" on this diversion to both Syria and Iraq. Turkey also offered to compensate her neighbors for the month long loss of Euphrates water by boosting the flow of the Euphrates from November until January.

In a meeting with this writer during the height of the tension, then-president of Turkey Turgut Ozal emphasized his commitment to resolve water disputes with Iraq and Syria, and acknowledged their concerns.

"I appreciate their fears," he said. "But we will not harm them. To the contrary, Turkey will more than make up for the water shortage. I have tried to convince Iraq and Syria of our positive intentions." As would be expected, however, Syria and Iraq reacted to the impoundment of Euphrates water with a surge of diplomatic cables, visits, and warnings.

The friction between Turkey, Syria, and Iraq over water access can only be defused through an explicit agreement among the three nations covering water allocations in the Tigris and Euphrates basins. But discussions have dragged on inconclusively since the 1960s. The Trilateral Committee on the Euphrates has met periodically, but has discussed mostly technical matters such as river flow rates and rainfall data. In the absence of a formal protocol on water basin management and apportionment, the World Bank and other multilateral lending agencies have withheld financial backing for Turkey's GAP project and related infrastructure.

Continued stalemate and the unilateral construction of new dams could lead to escalating disputes and confrontation. In 1975, Iraq and Syria came to the brink of war over Syria's reduction of the flow of the Euphrates to fill the Ath-Thawrah Dam, which Iraq claimed adversely affected 3 million Iraqi farmers. In 1986, there were reports that Turkey uncovered an alleged Syrian plot to blow up the Ataturk Dam (which Syria views as a direct threat to its farmers). In 1987, Ankara hinted that it might cut the flow of Euphrates water to Syria over Syrian support for Kurdish terrorists (the PKK) threatening the Turkish regime, an enduring source of tension between the two countries.

Syrian MIGs on "a training mission" shot down a Turkish survey plane, well within Turkey's borders, on October 21, 1989. Five people were killed in the incident.

Almost five years later, in January 1994, Turkish Prime Minister Tansu Ciller stated before a news conference, "I believe Syria could have helped in the struggle against terrorism, but it prefers not to. . . . The solution will be found when we manage to convince al-Assad that he will be better off without terrorism and that he will lose if he does not cooperate."

On November 20, 1993, an agreement was initialed between the head of the Syrian secret service and his Turkish counterpart for increased cooperation between the two countries. Turkey agreed to supply Syria's water requirements in return for Syrian promises to cooperate on the Kurdish problem. The agreement was endorsed by their respective foreign ministries in December 1993, and signed by their heads of state in April 1994.

Given the years of enmity between the two, one can reasonably question whether the agreement was written in invisible ink. One thing is clear: It was not the permanent agreement Syria was hoping for. If Syria accepted Turkey's offer for water sharing, it was because Syria badly needs the water and has no realistic chance of defeating Turkey in a military conflict over water in the years ahead.

Lebanon: Pearl or Oyster

In 1981, I dodged through a daily hail of bullets in Lebanon and shared underground shelters with Lebanese under fire. I ran in high-heeled sandals up mountain roads clogged with snow drifts and tanks, ate sandwiches of chocolate paste and tomatoes with baby-faced men in uniform, and slept through nights of shelling until it felt like a natural thing to do.

Evacuated by helicopter when the missiles could not be quieted, I returned again to race through militia checkpoints, where small boys pointed big guns to my forehead, demanding both camera and film.

Lebanon was once a shining light, where ever so briefly Christians, Muslims, and Jews lived in harmony. But that was before the PLO, expelled from Jordan in the Black September of 1970, overran the country, and before the protracted civil war that followed.

It was before the Iranian-sponsored Islamic Jihad terrorist attacks (both allegedly undertaken with Syrian complicity) on the American embassy in Beirut, where twelve Lebanese employees and seventeen U.S. diplomats lost their lives on April 18, 1983, and on the U.S. Marine compound, where over 241 American soldiers were killed on October 23, 1983.

And of course it was before the new Christian president, Bashir Gemayel, was blown to bits on September 14, 1982, by a huge bomb placed under his East Beirut headquarters, and—just when you thought it was almost over—Danny Chamoun, a voice for Lebanese independence, along with his wife and two children, were obliterated by gunfire in their home on October 21, 1990 (both acts with a trace of Syria in the powder).

And naturally it preceded the television reportage of the resident CIA station chief, William Buckley, having been taken hostage and bludgeoned to death in late 1984; of American hostages taken and freed an eternity of years later; and of Israeli soldiers captured and never freed—all purportedly at the hands of groups supported by Iran and Syria.

Lebanon: I, too, stood at the pinnacle of your majestic mountains in the blackness of midnight, mesmerized by the glittering, diamond lights of Beirut by the seashore below and—beyond the gallant, cresting waves of the Mediterranean—by the infinity of blinking stars above.

But that was before the U.S. government decided in

1992, after the Madrid Peace Conference, that preserving the freedom of Lebanon as an independent country was no longer worth the effort, and refused to intervene when the Syrians failed to implement their redeployment under the 1989 Taif Accords—thus consigning Lebanon to political servitude under Syrian masters. The Syrians knew all along that the strategic prize was theirs for the plucking; it was only a matter of patience, artillery, and time.

Lebanon is heralded in the Bible for cedar tree vistas and for King Hiram of Tyre, who provided all the cedar wood required for the building of King Solomon's temple. First settled nearly six thousand years ago by the ancient Phoenicians, the people of the sea, Lebanon is also a water-rich state, with eighteen major rivers. The country's 4 billion cubic meters of flowing water constitutes a treasure that could ideally be shared with regional neighbors under conditions of peace.

Substantial portions of the Litani River in the south have not been tapped and could be diverted to the Hasbani (Jordan River Basin), or to coastal cities like Beirut.

The Litani originates in the Syrian-controlled Bekaa Valley (an area infamous for drug-related activities), and flows south through the mountainous valley before turning west and flowing to the Mediterranean Sea. The river's largest withdrawal is diversion to the Awali River for power generation that serves Beirut and other coastal cities; 40 percent of Lebanon's electricity derives from Litani waters.

Lebanon's water supply and distribution systems were inadequate even as early as the 1950s. Direct hits suffered during the war years necessitate the creation of an entirely new network. The country's sewage system is overloaded, poorly maintained, and far from meeting basic sanitation requirements.

The country's numerous rivers and underground systems are recharged from bountiful rainfall and from snow accumulated high atop its mountains. A national engineering and management system, focused on the storage of this rain and snow water currently lost to the sea, could turn Lebanon into a Middle East water haven, were there the vision and stability to bring it to reality.

Instead, the country is crippled by severe water shortages in Beirut, seawater intrusion in the coastal aquifer, farmlands neglected for lack of irrigation water, and pipelines and aquifers severely damaged by war. Lebanon's sixteen years of civil and foreign-directed war resulted in more than $25 billion in overall damages.

The likelihood that Syria (and Iran) will voluntarily relinquish political control over Lebanon is no less fanciful, at the moment, than the prospect that Syria might encourage foreign investment in southern Lebanon's regional water potential.

Once renowned as the pearl of the Middle East, Lebanon today seems fated to remain a Syrian oyster.

13

SADDAM'S ATROCIOUS LITTLE WAR AGAINST THE GARDEN OF EDEN

Man marks the earth with ruin—
his control stops with the shore.
—Lord Byron,
"Childe Harold's Pilgrimage," 1812

I had it perfectly planned. I would fly from Washington's Dulles Airport to Charles de Gaulle in Paris for the connecting flight to Baghdad in May 1985. The four-hour layover would give me time to check into a nearby airport hotel, shower, catch two hours of rest, and emerge a reinvigorated person—ready for the long and uncertain journey ahead.

In Paris, an hour prior to the one P.M. departure time for my flight to Baghdad, I cheerfully boarded the minibus provided by the hotel and told the driver, "Iraqi Airlines, please."

"Mais madame," he responded. "Il ny'a pas Iraqi Airlines a Charles de Gaulle!" [There is no Iraqi Airlines at Charles de Gaulle!]

Alas, I was heading for the wrong airport, and the next flight to Iraq was three days away. The one-hour countdown to departure had begun. Orly (the right airport) was a fifty-five-minute drive away when there was no traffic, but twice that at midday. I threw my bags off the minibus, stood in the middle of the road madly waving my arms, and promised the first cab driver who stopped that I would pay him four times the regular fare if he could get me (and my bags) to the Iraqi Airlines counter at Orly in forty minutes.

Thirty-eight minutes later I entered Orly, which even on a slow day looks like an explosive device just went off, with everyone running for cover. There are two airports in the world that you "survive"—one being Cairo and the other Orly. Actually, they have much the same clientele, since Orly is the main transit point to the Middle East from Europe.

Fighting my way to the Iraqi Airlines counter, I found a young Iraqi woman sitting behind the reservations desk, but no passengers. "I'm on your flight to Baghdad," I said, madly waving my ticket.

"The flight to Baghdad departs in seven minutes," she responded, while slowly checking her computer, "but you are not confirmed for this flight." She returned to her magazine.

After an intense round of picturesque phrases, she relented. "Gate Seven. You have four minutes. Smoking or nonsmoking?" In the movies, the heroine leaps over the crowds, throws her bags on the X-ray machine, swoops them up again, and makes it to the plane with a minute to spare.

In real life, the journalist who leaps over crowds will more likely win the unwanted attention of omnipresent airport police. One must appear inconspicuous, preferably bored, while dashing through airport security.

I made it to the gate with seconds to spare, only to discover that the passengers were being forced to stand outside on the tarmac in the high summer sun, while being frisked and interrogated by Iraqi guards. "Why are you traveling to Baghdad?" the gendarmes demanded rather ungraciously, emptying the contents of my purse on the ground.

"That," I commented under my breath, "is an excellent question."

Break Dancing in Baghdad

Had you just flown in from outer space, or awakened from a ten-year sleep, you would have found few clues in Baghdad suggestive of a decade of war—prior that is, to Operation Desert Storm.

I was personally astonished to see a British tourist breakdancing on his head at the entrance to the now infamous El Rashid hotel. No one was paying attention, least of all the security guard.

Hard to believe? No more so than the passion in Iraq's capital for bowling, with slick new alleys available in almost every hotel. Or the sight of an American diplomat playing tennis in the searing midday sun "because otherwise you can never get a court."

Weddings took place every Thursday night, in a veritable dance of fashion that would have put Beirut to shame. Sixty-five newlywed couples celebrated during my stay, turning the marble-mausoleum hotel into a festival of music and haute cuisine.

The quality of life for most Baghdadis wasn't bad at all. In fact, the average workday in Baghdad didn't look much different from the routine nine-to-five in Baltimore or Cleveland.

Western fashion was "in" in Iraq. The heavy black Moslem chador was rarely seen on the streets of Baghdad. A monthly magazine published by the Federation of Iraqi Women featured special articles on fashion and makeup for the working woman that bore striking resemblance to pieces out of *Mademoiselle*.

Soldiers were "advised" not to wear their uniforms in the city if they could avoid doing so. "We don't like people to be reminded of the war all the time," an official explained. Even the internal police tended to keep a low public profile, although they magically appeared in force, armed with grenades, if one happened to snap a picture without authorization.

A construction wave of new buildings and boulevards was launched by Saddam Hussein prior to the Iran war, in order to give Baghdad a modern face. Western-style high-rise office and apartment buildings were rising all over town.

A new Iraqi flat typically has three bedrooms, and cost (prior to the embargo) between $75,000 and $100,000. This was not out of reach for the average white-collar worker, who earned between $600 and $1,000 a month, paid no taxes, and was the likely recipient of a low-interest government mortgage.

Hotel lounges were a popular romantic refuge, with young lovers holding hands for hours over espresso—perhaps the penultimate contrast between secular Iraq and her fundamentalist enemy, Iran. And for those so inclined, the government had built a rest haven thirty miles from Baghdad, replete with bungalows, golf courses, several restaurants, and even a discotheque for the younger set.

The goal was to keep spirits high, as far as public funds could be stretched. If Iraqis were being forced to face the trauma of war and austerity, the Ba'athist regime wanted to ensure that people enjoyed themselves in the process—at least from time to time.

During Desert Storm, however, few Iraqis were dancing. Within a year after the war's conclusion, two-thirds of Iraqi children had become malnourished due to limited food supplies, and half of the country's citizens had been exposed to drinking water contaminated by the waste of combat. For the first time in Iraqi history, waterborne diseases reached epidemic proportions, with hepatitis alone up one hundredfold.

The war debris reportedly included accidentally released radioactive substances, left to sow death in the aquifers of Babylon and beyond.

At least fifty-three thousand Iraqi civilians died *after* the Gulf War—from hunger, waterborne diseases, and uprisings against the regime—as compared to three thousand to five thousand civilian deaths during the war. By mid-1994, most Iraqis were barely protected from starvation by the state-run rationing system, while some were eating only once a day.[1]

Chlorine sources and aluminum sulfate factories were hit by allied bombing, along with electrical power and fuel plants, with the result that five hundred sites in Baghdad were left ankle-deep in sewage. Seven large regulators directing the flow of the Tigris and Euphrates, as well as several large dams on the Euphrates, were also damaged.

By the close of 1994, Islamic fundamentalism had gained strong footholds in quarantined Iraq. The discos were closed, and music could no longer be heard drifting through the streets.

Trying to Raise the Birthrate, Not Lower It

One striking measure of the changes in Iraqi society caused by the previous Iraq/Iran war was the enhanced role of Iraqi women. With several hundred thousand men away at the front, and another several hundred thousand on call for the better part of a decade, women kept the machinery of the government and the economy running. Posts at the highest technical levels of engineering and science were held by women, and in many government offices they outnumbered men by four to one.

The Ba'ath Socialist Party made equality between the sexes an important part of its political agenda from the time it assumed power in the late 1960s. By 1980, Iraq had already surpassed most Arab countries on this issue, with women accounting for almost a quarter of the labor force, including more than 30 percent of teachers and doctors, 25 percent of physicists, and almost half of the workers in the agricultural sector.

Secular steps taken since 1980 to advance the position of Iraqi women and to utilize their talents in the workforce were especially significant when viewed against the background of the Muslim religion. More than 55 percent of Iraq's population is Shiite, and 40 percent Sunni.

Iraqi divorce laws give custody of children under the age

of fourteen to the mother, whereas women have no rights to custody under a Muslim divorce. In Iraq, a man can no longer divorce his wife without her consent, and it is now the husband who must move out of the home. The house, almost sacrosanct within the Muslim faith as the essence of manhood, reverts back to his possession only upon the wife's remarriage, or several years after the divorce if she does not remarry.

Iraq will have as many as 49 million people by 2025. Yet the solution to Iraq's "population crisis"—in the leadership's view—is to find a way to rapidly *increase* the country's population. Iraq's leaders fear that surrounding countries will be able to achieve dominance due to their high birthrates. Bordering nations Iran and Turkey each already claim well over 60 million people, with Syria close to 14 million. According to UN high projections, Turkey could reach a population of 101 million by 2025, Iran 150 million, and Syria almost 38 million.

As a consequence, Iraqi women could find themselves pedaling backward over the next ten years, rather than ahead. "The birthrate is a matter on which we cannot budge," stated a senior Iraqi official.

Iraq's present population exceeds 20 million people, but only about 30 percent are actually in the labor force (most at skeletal wages compared to former pay scales). A major part of Iraq's population is under the age of fifteen—one of the highest ratios of children in the Arab world. An estimated 1.5 million Iraqis have found sanctuary in exile.

Approximately 750,000 men are in the Iraqi standing army—some estimates put it at over a million, or nearly a fourth of the labor force. This has previously resulted in manpower shortages so severe that the regime was forced to bring in over 2 million foreign workers by the beginning of the 1980s.

Food Psychosis

Both the Iran and Persian Gulf wars created a virtual food psychosis in Baghdad, a race to achieve agricultural independence and self-sufficiency.

Until 1973, Iraq was a relatively poor country. The Arab oil embargo following the Yom Kippur war, along with escalating oil prices, created newfound wealth for the Ba'athist regime. When the Iran War began in 1980, Iraq was rich and debt-free.

Five years later, her foreign exchange reserves of $35 billion were depleted, external debt had reached $20 billion, and payments due to foreign governments and companies had to be rescheduled. Exports had dropped by over $19 billion—from $26 billion to $7 billion—by 1983.

Iraq still claimed the second-largest oil reserves in the world after Saudi Arabia, but the oil embargo and uncertainty over future oil prices had unalterably changed the economic terrain as far as the leadership was concerned. By the mid-1980s, the machinery of state was dedicated to "diversification" of the industrial and agricultural sectors, with the goal of untying the economy from the price of oil.

Agricultural development was accorded highest priority. Prior to the Gulf War, the agricultural sector was already employing almost 35 percent of the population (as compared to 3 percent in oil production), and it alone provided sufficient employment for Iraq's increasingly youthful population.

Iraq's leaders have long believed that the country could achieve as much revenue from agricultural exports as it once did from oil. Prior to the Gulf War, crude oil accounted for 99 percent of Iraq's merchandise exports, while the country imported over 60 percent of its food supply.

The austerity program launched in 1993, and the post–Gulf War embargo, resulted in exorbitant prices for many locally produced goods, and bare market shelves. Such experiences have created such an obsessive atmosphere around issues of food that, for Iraq, agricultural self-sufficiency has become synonymous with national security. Iraqis are determined that foreign powers will never again be in a position to dictate whether or what they eat.

The country is rich in land: 433,000 square kilometers, all of it cultivable. The key is freshwater sources. The lower Euphrates and 68 percent of Iraq's irrigated lands are highly saline. Moreover, even partial fulfillment of development plans by Turkey and Syria will make it difficult for Iraq to meet its own irrigation needs on the Euphrates.

Although nearly three-quarters of the Tigris-Euphrates river basin lies within Iraq, more than 80 percent of the country's water is at the mercy of its upstream neighbors, Turkey, Syria, and to a lesser extent, Iran. Future depletion estimates on the Euphrates range from 30 to 40 percent by Turkey and 20 to 30 percent by Syria (based on completion of Turkey's GAP project and projected Syrian withdrawals).

Turkish officials contend that Iraq's fear is unfounded, since it would be technically impossible for Turkey to close the water tap. A lack of shared technical data and neutral analysis has been a glaring omission in the debate.

In an average year, the Euphrates' capacity is estimated by the World Bank at 31.82 billion cubic meters, a quantity which can satisfy the demands of Turkey, Syria, and Iraq. In 1989, the flow fell to 16.87 billion cubic meters, the lowest in a half-century, causing serious water shortages in all three countries. Approximately 10 percent of the annual flow to Iraq is also lost via evaporation from Turkish reservoirs.

Iraq's pragmatic approach has been to exploit the relatively cleaner, more abundant, and secure Tigris river, along with its northern and eastern tributaries. The Tigris and its tributaries, it should be noted, lie close to Iraq's northern Kurdish region—perhaps another reason for the regime to try to rid itself of the Kurdish population.

But the bulk of Iraqi agriculture, along with most of its population, is located in the southern and central regions of the state. Further expansion therefore requires extensive population relocation, and the retention of northern Tigris waters.

Iraq had hoped to turn its economic advantage, oil, into the foundation for an industrially and scientifically based economy. Oil pipelines through Saudi Arabia and Turkey could produce annual oil revenues of about $20 billion. But even this income would be insufficient to underwrite the regime's development goals.

"We should be courageous enough to admit we have difficulties," the Iraqi undersecretary of oil told this writer prior to the Gulf War. "If we do not act in a bold manner, valuable time will be lost and our targets won't be met." Iraq squandered that valuable time, along with the deep pocket of Arab aid, when it invaded Kuwait in September 1990. Arab financial assistance to Iraq had reached $50 billion in the decade prior to the Persian Gulf conflict.

Gratitude, however, was never part of the equation. Iraq perceived itself as the great fortress of the Arab world, leading the charge in a thousand-year battle with the Persian Empire. From this perspective, Arab aid was a duty, a dire responsibility, but hardly an act of benevolence.

"Frankly," explained an expert on the country, "it is hard to imagine what someone would have to do to make the Iraqis feel grateful for anything, given their history, their intensely independent nature, and their isolated position on the eastern flank."

"Think of the mentality of a people who see no future," another Iraq-watcher commented. "When a milk cow stops giving milk, you kill it."

"We Drink Nothing but Germs, Worms, and Bitterness"

It is a rare journalist who risks his "objective" reputation to champion *invisible* victims of mass slaughter. Michael Woods, a BBC journalist, did just that with his 1993 investigation into atrocities against southern Iraq's marsh Arabs —a strategy of genocide directly linked to Iraq's race for food security, and a tragedy still largely ignored by the world press.

"Since the end of the Gulf War and the failed uprising against Saddam Hussein, a terrible human tragedy is unfolding here in the marshes on the border of southern Iraq and Iran," Michael Woods stated in a public television documentary on February 27, 1994.

"The Shia faith arose in the Biblical Garden of Eden, the land of the two rivers, Tigris and Euphrates, whose waters nourished the first civilization on earth," said Woods. "Surrounded by the palm forest of the Euphrates, Kerbala lies in the plain of Southern Iraq. . . . At the end of the Gulf War, encouraged by President Bush, the Shia rose against Saddam's tyranny and here, at Kerbala, Saddam took savage revenge."

This, in brief, is the plot: Tigris waters nurture the rich

southern marshlands of Iraq. The marsh Arabs, a culture that dates back to the first civilization on earth, are Shia, and not of the ruling Sunni Muslim religious clan. Thus, the extermination of marsh Arabs through the draining of their swamplands is of little human consequence to the Iraqi regime.

During their 1991 uprising, Kurdish forces captured Saddam's police headquarters in Erbil, along with its immense security archive. A memo was found that sheds unequivocal light on the government's marshland policy.

The document read:

> Strategic security operations such as poisoning, that means poisoning the marshwater, explosions, that means dynamiting the installations and the burning of houses will be conducted against subversives in the marsh areas. . . .
>
> The principle of economic blockade must be applied to the marsh villages through the withdrawal of all food supply agencies, through a ban on the sale of fish, by taking the severest measures against persons who smuggle food into the marshes, launches operating in the marshes must be totally banned . . . and consideration must be given to the possibility of regrouping the marsh villages on dry land which is easy to control and opening roads and points of access into the heart of the marshes.

A map was also captured that detailed the plan to drain the marshes and divert the water through massive dikes into a huge canal.

The marsh Arabs have harvested the reed beds, fished, and tended their water buffalo here since the dawn of history. But after the 1991 uprisings, the Iraqis put their marsh plan into action. "Burning, shelling, deporting the people, poisoning the water, everything they said they would do, they did," Woods emphasized.

The marsh lakes and streams are now choking on putrefied fish in a deliberately engineered environmental and cultural catastrophe. There were no cameras to report the initial atrocities; only smuggled amateur video footage showed vast tracks of the marshes in death's grasp. In smuggled footage, taken in mid-1993, the marshes were nearly dry.

The Iraqi government, according to Woods, "told the U.N. this was all part of an agricultural improvement scheme."

On desperate placards set up for Woods's camera, people still trapped inside this "scheme" asked simply for life and for water—the lifeblood of the marshes. One placard read "We drink nothing but germs, worms, and bitterness." Another sign cried out: "We beg God and we beg you. They have blocked off the waters of the Amara marshes from us. If you have any mercy, just let us have water. Why don't the American planes bomb the dikes and release water for us? We have been held to ransom. We are saturated with suffering. We are saturated with shame. Do you accept our humiliation?"

Max Van Der Stoel, UN Human Rights Special Rapporteur on Iraq, described the marsh massacres as "one of the most serious cases of massive violation of human rights we have seen since the Second World War."

At the close of his documentary, Woods conducted an interview with a high-ranking Clinton administration official. "We have looked at a lot of options in the south of Iraq . . . and to see whether we could do more on the ground that would be helpful to the marsh Arabs," the responsible official stated. "Unfortunately, . . . it's proved very difficult, I'd say impossible, to set up a safe-haven type arrangement."

Bombing the canals is not feasible, he explained, "partly because of the way in which they're built, but also because the Iraqi army is very good at engineering and they—we're not talking about a dam here—they would rebuild it very quickly within twenty-four to forty-eight hours. So that a lot of those options are just not viable options unfortunately."

One is hard-pressed to fathom how Iraqi engineers could prove more imaginative and capable than America's finest fighter pilots, or that a large canal could be rebuilt in twenty-four hours. Indeed, it took the Iraqis two years to refill the reservoirs of dams hit by allied bombing during the Gulf War. (The Bush administration, it should be noted, swiftly deployed nearly fifty thousand U.S. troops to Kuwait, when Iraqi forces amassed on its border in October 1994.)

"Is there *nothing* the outside world can do for these people and for a waterland that rests at the core of our cultural heritage?" Marsh again inquired.

"Well, we can bear witness," the official replied.

But bear witness to what? As the marshes of Eden lie vanquished, Saddam Hussein is still president, trade sanctions have lost their bite, and businessmen are again hungering for "golden deals" just over Iraq's horizon.[2]

To the Realm of Power: In Summary

"I am only one, but still I am one," wrote Edward Everett Hale in *The Man Without a Country* (1863). "I cannot do everything, but still I can do something."

If left to the powerful, the Promised Land will soon be covered by concrete, with little trace remaining of the life-giving mustard seed. Israel's coastal aquifer will no longer be salvageable, and the mountain aquifer, on which the Palestinians pin their future, could become the refuse dump of progress.

Hastily devised engineering schemes will deplete the precious earth and waters of the ancient Negev and Dead Sea areas, but fill the coffers of corporations and politicians. Ill-begotten tourism projects, heralded as the harbingers of lasting peace, could prove the gate of no return for the Gulf of Aqaba/Eilat, the Red Sea waters between Jordan and Israel.

Left to the powerful, Israel will eventually concede almost a third of its present water supply to Syrian dominion, and a major portion of the remainder to Palestinian rule—but with no apparent alternative in place. The Hashemite Kingdom of Jordan, irrespective of water agreements with Israel, will disappear into the encroaching desert sands, if it is forgotten by the international community; the Syrian people will continue to suffer from the misguided water policies of their leaders; Lebanon's water promise will remain unfulfilled; Iraq will complete its genocide against the marsh Arabs; and hunger could stalk the paradise of Eden.

III

TO THE PROMISE

14

CARETAKERS AND REDEEMERS

The politics of life is personal initiative, creativity, flair, a little daring. The politics of death is calculation, prudence, measured gestures.
—R. Sargent Shriver, on receiving the American Medal of Freedom, August 8, 1994

We were told at the beginning," said Oren Lyons, chief of the Onondaga Indian Nation, "that as long as we continue our ceremonies—one to speak, one to dance, and one to listen—then we will have water. But when we stop our speaking, our dancing, and our listening, the water will be gone."

The chief was speaking before a convocation of the world's foremost political and business leadership, gathered in the shimmering snow town of Davos, Switzerland, for the 1992 World Economic Forum.

"We know this time is coming," he continued. " 'The message is: it will happen. All we can do is buy time for the coming generations, who look up from the earth, waiting their turn. Everyone knows that we're moving toward a point of no return, but no one slows down. We only accelerate.' "

There was stony silence in the audience, when a man slowly rose from his chair to ask, "How can you proclaim such a message of hopelessness? We don't want to hear that. Why should we care about a better world if it is only a matter of time?"

The chief smiled sadly. "For future generations looking up from the earth and awaiting their turn," he said, "time is a crucial gift."

The American Redeemer

The people of the Middle East look to the international community in general, and to the United States in particular, to help them overcome scarce and polluted waters. Yet, the U.S. record in this arena remains cloudy.

The United States holds the world leadership in defining acceptable water quality for human consumption, but the Center for Disease Control reported over 40,000 cases of water-borne diarrheal diseases in 1988.

Some ground water in the United States is so heavily contaminated that even state-of-the-art technologies cannot clean it to the point where it is drinkable, according to a study released in June 1994 by the National Research Council. Focusing on seventy-seven cases, the study determined that full cleanup was possible in only eight.

In the next thirty years an estimated $1 trillion could be spent on attempts to clean U.S. groundwater sites. Of the 300,000 to 400,000 such contaminated sites across the United States, some can again be made potable; but in many others, complete cleanup is just not technically feasible.[1]

"The drinking water program is in shambles," said Representative Henry Waxman, the California Democrat who then chaired the House Subcommittee on Health and Environment, in a 1991 interview.[2] Environmental writer Jessica Mathews described the environmental record of the 103rd Congress as "pure scorched earth," noting that reauthorization and needed improvements to the Clean Water Act and the Safe Drinking Water Act had all failed.[3]

The state of the Rio Grande, the most contaminated water body in the United States, could ultimately affect Americans from Maine to California. ABC's *World News Tonight* reported on December 22, 1992, that the Rio Grande at the Texas border is a "cesspool" nurturing a burgeoning epidemic of hepatitis, liver disease, and cholera, all of which could spread across the country through interconnected groundwater systems, leading to human "catastrophe" on an unprecedented scale. Dr. Bernard Craun of the National Centers for Disease Control stated that a regional problem of this type could well become a national epidemic.

The poisoning of American underground water systems knows no boundaries. Thus, when Sandia Laboratories in New Mexico buries radioactive substances that eventually seep into the groundwater system of Albuquerque, these same toxic substances could one day end up in the milk of children in Iowa, Maine, or Alaska.

On April 8, 1993, the U.S. Government Accounting Office issued a report condemning the Environmental Protection Agency for doing a "poor job of inspecting public water supply systems . . . and ensuring that sanitary programs are consistently implemented." We need look no further than Milwaukee for confirmation: Most of the drinking water there was contaminated and thousands took ill from a mere "intestinal parasite" that accidentally found its way into the water supply that same year.

A community in Alabama, as well as many others

throughout the nation, had thousands of tons of DDT released into their water supplies over the course of a period of years.

For twenty years hospitals in the Syracuse area have been dumping their medical wastes on the Onandaga Indian Nation territory. According to a 1992 EPA assessment, dozens of fifty-five-gallon drums full of wastes, as well as hundreds of garbage bags containing used bandages, syringes, and other unidentified material, were scattered along a creek next to Quarry Road in the Onandaga territory. Residents said that children playing along the creek found human remains.

Drinking water, not lead paint, accounts for 15 to 25 percent of American children's intake of lead—and more if the water is contaminated. Nine percent of all bladder cancers in the United States (about 4,200 cases) and 15 percent of all rectal cancers (about 6,000 cases) are thought to be caused by long-term consumption of chlorinated waters.

Water-borne radon may cause more cancer deaths than all other drinking-water contaminants combined. The EPA estimates that at least 80 million people have high amounts of radon in their water supply.

International Mission Almost Impossible

International environmental disasters such as the Gulf War oil fires, contamination of Lake Baikal in Russia (the deepest freshwater lake in the world), and the dangerous pollution of the Danube and the Rhine, are just the tip of the proverbial iceberg.

International organizations such as UNICEF, the United Nations Development Programme, the United Nations Environment Programme, and the World Health Organization, as well as the aid agencies of the leading Western nations, invest much of their resources attempting to stem the suffering. Nevertheless, approximately 40 percent of the world's rural population and nearly 200 million urban residents are still denied access to safe drinking water; 1.7 billion do not have access to adequate sanitation facilities—a figure that has not declined in thirteen years.

Despite the fact that the United Nations declared the 1980s the "Drinking Water and Sanitation Decade," contaminated waters remain the source of almost 80 percent of the illnesses that ravage third world countries; 40 percent of the people of the African continent is at risk of water-related disease and death by the turn of the century.

As many as thirty-five thousand children die every day from thirst or water contamination. Technologies that can help rectify the problem are well known; financial and institutional support, however, is sorely lacking.

When raw sewage infiltrated city pipes in New Delhi, for example, the tap water suddenly became black, foul-smelling, and thick like sewage. "One minute my baby was laughing and playing, and then she was dead," a young mother told the press.[4]

"Water, water everywhere, but not a drop to drink," lamented Coleridge's ancient mariner. If energy were free, we could use existing technology to remove the dissolved salts present in seawater and adapt water quality to any desired use. But energy is far from free.

Today poor people in both rich and developing nations are the most severely affected by water contamination; tomorrow, the most affluent communities in the richest countries will suffer the curse of our ignorance.

"All these aid organizations came in and told women

they should boil their water, but nobody stopped to ask the women how many sticks they've got to put in the fire to boil the water," said a CARE representative of India. "To boil one liter of water for twenty minutes uses up their entire day's supply of fuel."[5]

Protection and maintenance of basic water and sanitation infrastructure around the globe is a matter of deadly urgency. China's seven major rivers are choked with sewage and industrial waste; in the Indian state of West Bengal, almost six hundred thousand people draw their water from wells containing arsenic at three times the permissible level (by UN standards) for human consumption; in Russia, where almost every large river is polluted by industrial waste and agricultural runoff, many cities report that their drinking water reeks of gasoline.[6]

Further international examples of neglect, irresponsibility, and havoc abound. In April 1992, for example, the Colombian government declared a state of economic emergency due in large part to incompetence and corruption in maintaining the country's reservoirs. The very same month, gasoline leaks caused by the negligence of a major corporation caused at least nine explosions in a mile-long corridor of sewer systems in Guadalajara, Mexico, claiming six hundred lives and destroying more than one thousand buildings; and the Chicago River broke through a wall that should have been repaired weeks earlier, and brought Chicago's downtown area to a standstill, causing over a billion dollars' worth of damage.

The most compelling commentary on the Chicago debacle was the response of the transportation official responsible for overseeing repairs. Questioned by investigators, the official admitted that he had failed to carry out required safety inspections because he could never find a parking space near the wall.

Thundering at Rio: But Little Water

In June 1992, thirty thousand environmentalists thundered their way to Rio de Janeiro for the first United Nations Earth Summit. Among them were three thousand presidents, prime ministers, and ministerial minions. Hundreds of millions of dollars were spent on the exercise; a feverish round of preliminary conferences was held daily all over the world, and complete forests were denuded in paperwork alone.

An Earth Charter was signed in Rio, signaling a crescendo in man's acknowledgment of his debt to nature. Commitments of humility poured forth from the cups of power. Yet, for all the fiery talk about the environment and our precious resources, the political and economic restructuring essential to stave off calamity remains at odds with the political priorities and will of the majority of world leaders.

The United Nations spent several million dollars just on a series of major international water conferences leading up to the Rio summit. Notwithstanding, the outpouring of reports and recommendations, the water crisis was barely dealt with on the Rio agenda, let alone defined as a fundamental priority.

UN Secretary General Boutros Boutros-Ghali was recently asked by this author about the prospect of UN leadership on water issues. "The United Nations is a weak institution," he sighed. "It can intervene to try to stop wars and conflict once they begin, but can do very little to prevent conflict or environmental catastrophe that could lead to war."

"You see," he continued, "it is relatively easy to negotiate a treaty to end a conflict between warring parties. But to negotiate a water-sharing treaty, that is a much greater challenge. The war treaty comes after five thousand people have died. The water treaty may save five hundred thousand lives."

Author and *Washington Post* business editor David Ignatius provided astute commentary on the role of conferences among the "merit class" of decision-makers. "The discussions weren't supposed to settle anything," wrote Ignatius.[7] "That isn't the name of the game in conferenceland. The goal is to discuss issues, not resolve them. . . . Indeed, strong beliefs are almost a liability in this setting. They get in the way. They make for awkward moments at cocktail hour.

"You've heard so many earnest speeches over the years that you honestly don't believe any of them any more," he continued. "The part of you that believes in things—that would take action to deal with them—gets worn down."

The meritocratic approach to water crises is exemplified in the dozens of UN and other international conferences held between 1991 and 1994 on the future of the Aral Sea. The sea, located primarily in Kazakhstan, has shrunk by half, and is expected to disappear in twenty years time, due to a Soviet irrigation project that turned Uzbekistan into the world's third-largest cotton producer.

Despite endless speeches of concern, however, no local or international body has yet taken a decisive first step to reverse the sea's decline. In fact, just as the momentous UN–sponsored Cairo Population Conference was concluding, global environmentalists meeting in Uzbekistan announced on September 8, 1994, that they had "suspended their efforts to save the Aral Sea . . . and begun simpler, stopgap measures to combat a related health crisis." International agencies were unlikely to begin serious rehabilitation work on the sea for several decades, the press was told. By that time, the Aral Sea, once the fourth-largest inland body of water, would be a third of its original size, and likely split into three smaller seas.[8]

A recent secret internal report on the World Bank's water policies acknowledged that, while the bank had helped resolve a dispute between Pakistan and India on the Indus River thirty years ago, "in subsequent years the Bank and other organizations have not placed emphasis on proactive, facilitating roles in promoting the systematic planning and management of international water resources."

The World Bank has lent over $17 billion for irrigation and drainage projects over the last twenty years. Yet only 50 percent of the bank's irrigation projects in 1989 were deemed satisfactory by an internal audit. In 1990, the figure dropped to less than 50 percent. The bank's internal water policy review also noted that World Bank water projects are plagued by a host of serious problems, including lack of accountability and failure to address water resource issues in a comprehensive manner.

A senior World Bank official recently resigned in protest over bank plans to finance a $770 million project in large-scale dam and road construction in the pristine valley of the Himalaya Mountains in northern Nepal. The bank official, as well as leading environmentalists, claim that the Arun Valley dam would put the economic future and quality of life of the Nepalese people at risk.[9]

"There was no vision at the top on this issue," said an official close to the inner workings of the bank. "I could see this on a daily basis. Everybody worked in his own little cell."

The bank seems lately to be moving in a more constructive and "culturally sensitive" direction. By mid-1993, critics of the World Bank had positive reviews for the new president, Lou Preston, and his willingness to listen and to seriously examine past bank mistakes. A revitalized World Bank water policy has been crafted, although many of the assumptions that guided the bank in earlier decades are still firmly in place.

Unfortunately, there is no single, broad-brush solution to the international water challenge. Some water experts have lobbied for the establishment of an International Water Authority under the aegis of the United Nations. Staffed by the very same exhausted people who run existing water agencies, the IWA would prove a weak guarantor of national responsibility or political will.

Politicians and national leaders who appreciate the role of water in our lives, and who actually champion its cause, are sorrowfully few. For water resources are typically the privileged domain of governments and politicians at the highest level, who haven't the time to care. Environmentalists can hardly salvage the planet while our planetary leaders sacrifice the water that gives it life.

How ironic that Japan, host to the environmental multilateral forum of the Madrid peace process, waged an international press campaign before and after the Rio summit for the right to transport hazardous nuclear material across three oceans.

Russia, co-convener of the 1991 Madrid Peace Conference, towed nearly two thousand tons of low-level radioactive waste toward a dump site in the Sea of Japan in October 1993—in violation of Russia's own laws, not to mention an international moratorium on dumping that Russia had vowed to uphold.

Let us also recall that Norway, facilitator of the 1993 Israeli-Palestinian peace accord, readily pointed to this achievement as justification for its right to slaughter an increased number of whales, a mammal custodian of our seas.

Environmental activists can hardly be expected to shoulder responsibility for ensuring pure and plentiful water reserves in a national and international leadership vacuum.

"The problem is that those entrusted to save the planet are exhausted, burned out," declared Noel Brown, deputy director of the United Nations Environment Programme, with rare candor. Environmentalists are pulled in so many directions, he said, that what they most long for "is simply sleep."[10]

Food Security: Not on the Agenda

"Not one agricultural system in the developing world will be able to produce as much food as needed," said Robert O. Blake, chairman of the Committee on Agricultural Sustainability for Developing Countries, "without destroying its own system."[11]

Short of a committed educational campaign to help the American and international public comprehend that our very survival is at stake, the folly of food insecurity could be turned into yet another weapon pitting nation against nation in the coming century.

Agricultural development must, of course, be balanced with environmental planning. A large segment of the environmentalist community views agriculture as inherently disruptive of the ecosystem.

Ann Thrupp, director of sustainable agriculture at the World Resources Institute's Center for International Development and Environment, argues that food security and resource degradation are closely connected. Declining yields lead to low productivity, which in turn leads to lack of food.

Since the food and health of our people depend on the agricultural base, we desperately need a wise mediator to help strike a compromise between the two camps.

Efforts to draw congressional attention to the global food emergency have until now sparked little enthusiasm. "We have been bombarding Congress for years with statistics," Robert Blake told participants in a 1992 Environmental and Energy Study Institute briefing on Capitol Hill, "but the results are a big yawn, a big zero."

Members of Congress, he said, view agriculture as "business as usual," or convince themselves "that there is a big revolution in food production just around the corner." Neither assumption is correct. Fifteen to twenty years from now, said Blake, "Our grandchildren will ask, 'Where were we when we could have done something about it?' "

Although 5 million American children go hungry each month, and almost 30 million adults and children do not have enough to eat, food security is hardly a concern for most Americans. Yet, as documented by the U.S. Conference of Mayors, the demand for emergency food in major U.S. cities has been spiraling annually since 1983, with an 18-percent surge in 1992 alone.

The number of families with children requesting assistance in 1992 leapt forward by 14 percent compared to 1991. A national survey by Catholic Charities, U.S.A. found that six out of ten people they served in 1990 required emergency food or shelter, up dramatically from two out of ten a decade earlier. By January 1993, the nation's food-stamp program was feeding 26.8 million people.

The last hundred thousand years have been a period of remarkable climate stability. Today, however, we face disruptive temperature rises over land. The U.S. corn belt, currently producing 200 million tons of corn a year, or one-eighth of the world harvest, is seriously threatened. Each year the United States exports approximately 100 million tons to a hundred countries around the world; but world grain reserves have plummeted, while grain prices are accelerating, and could even triple in the coming years.

Blake believes it will take the shock of massive numbers of people dying all over the world to move the American public. "People don't understand the problem," he said, "nor the relationship to American interests."

Growing Money Versus Food

The first step in defining those interests, Blake stated, would be to call hunger by its modern name, food security. Terminology that bespeaks aid and food relief, rather than reform, is a relic of the past.

Congressman Tony Hall of Ohio went on a three week water-only fast in April 1993 to protest the abolition of the House Hunger Committee, which he headed, and to elevate the issue of hunger on the policy agenda. Hall pressed for three new policy initiatives: a "national summit on hunger," a UN convention "on the right to food," and a new congressional body focused on hunger.

The U.S. Department of Agriculture responded by agreeing to host a series of five national hunger summits, the first on June 17, 1993. Hundreds of experts and activists were in attendance at this meeting, which President Clinton addressed.

In addition, John W. Stanton, a former Republican congressman from Ohio and an adviser to the World Bank, quickly convinced the bank to host a series of international hunger summits, bringing visibility to an inexplicably invisible issue. Ironically, however, the World Bank has neither a unit nor even a specialist specifically tasked to deal with hunger or food security. The unofficial bank position is that food security per se is a nonissue.

Indeed, it is the nongovernmental organizations (NGOs) that tend to work the hardest in the poorest parts of the world to try to teach people how better to capture water, grow alternative crops, and store their food. "The NGOs teach them how to grow food, and we teach them how to grow money," said a World Bank adviser.

A senior bank agricultural economist suggested to this writer that food security can indeed be achieved as long as three conditions are in place: world production can meet world demand; people have the financial means to acquire food; and there are no major sociopolitical obstacles to international trade. The great caveat, he acknowledged, is population control. "Obviously you cannot increase population to infinity," the adviser stated, "unless *Star Trek* means to colonize other planets are devised."

According to his theoretical approach, decisions on food crop production should be made, like all other economic decisions, on the basis of comparative advantage. Thus, national planners would determine whether their country would be better off producing more maize for domestic consumption or producing and exporting more clothes or microchips in order to import their maize.

United Nations Food and Agricultural Organization (FAO) statistics tend to demonstrate, he said, that in principle, notwithstanding local or regional shortages, there is no overall lack of food in the world. More could be produced, though at varying costs in different places, and at rapidly prohibitive costs in other places. "The problem is one of sitting down in each case and deciding what is the most appropriate use of land, water, human, and financial resources," said the World Bank economist. Food security, according to this line of reasoning, is a derivative of financial security.

This linear approach assumes liberal trade and investments in alternative, more profitable, sources of income where land and water are major constraints. However, the old adage about teaching a person to fish rather than providing benevolent aid is effective as long as the subject lives by the sea, and the sea carries fish. People on the seaside of Africa are discouraged from fishing because the cost of imported meat from Europe is so cheap. Confronted by foreign competition, local fishermen, as well as farmers, simply stop producing. So we now have rich countries selling more meat to poorer countries, which turns local producers into the poorer people who buy the meat.

In reality, the majority of our global population lives in places with limited potential to grow food, but knows little about doing anything else. Sixty percent of the world's people and about half of the arable land of the planet is currently employed in agriculture. The human percentage escalates to 80 percent of the labor force in the poorest developing countries. Yet economists tend to overlook or dismiss the cultural and social value of agriculture in developing countries.

In Turkey, for example, where 50 percent of the population is engaged in agriculture, the government relies on "cost-ineffective" policies where necessary in order to raise income levels in rural areas. Thus the Turkish government purchases crude tobacco from farmers whose ancestors have been growing it for hundreds of years, rather than bring welfare to those rural areas, or attract the farmers to overburdened cities. The tobacco cannot be exported, and people in other parts of the country don't want to buy it.

To convince the farmers to grow an alternative crop, however, would threaten an extended-family culture built around this particular tobacco.

"We tell them to shift to lentils," said one official, "but their tobacco is a way of life." Instead, the government simply destroys the tobacco.

Dedicated liberalism would further provide for the freedom of people to move across national boundaries in search of food. But as Rwanda, Somalia, Yugoslavia, and the central Soviet Republics so vividly demonstrate, tribal, ethnic, and nation-state hatreds are unlikely to be supplanted in the foreseeable future by universal understanding and brotherly sustenance.

The 1993 World Refugee Survey, a report by the U.S. Committee for Refugees, indicates that there are currently 17.5 million refugees adrift in the world, while the "internally displaced" (a totally separate category) account for approximately 24 million. Carnegie Endowment refugee expert Demetrios Papa Demetrios believes that if ethnic conflicts and environmental disasters are factored into our calculations, the numbers of refugees and internally displaced "could increase geometrically." Refugee numbers have fluctuated by 10 or 20 percent to either side of 15 million for the past ten years, while the number of internally displaced has virtually "exploded."

The Middle East Food Horizon

If Middle East and U.S. policy-makers continue to stare blankly at the food security horizon, we could be talking about food-war—rather than water-war—scenarios in the coming millennium.

The United Nation estimates that more than 50 percent of agricultural land in developing countries has been degraded by the erosion of 24 billion tons of soil annually—an amount equivalent to all the topsoil on Australia's wheat land. Yet there is no global monitoring system in place.

Only the United States knows how much topsoil it is losing each year. The 1985 U.S. Farm Bill required American farmers to reduce the country's losses by one-third. The United States could easily lead the international charge in establishing capability for the scientific monitoring of soil erosion.

The United States should promote partnerships between Middle Eastern and American researchers in advanced agricultural research. Agricultural research is one of the most effective tools for coping with water scarcity, costs of future sources of water, food security, and environmental protection. The failure to stimulate private-sector involvement in agricultural research, said one expert, "is gross negligence."

The United States became irresponsibly complacent about food supplies in the 1980s, when it cut its investments in the agricultural potential of developing countries. The U.S. National Extension Service, which helps transmit technology to farmers across the globe, is short on funds and vision.

U.S.–sponsored agricultural programs around the world remain marginal, Robert Blake believes, largely in deference to the domestic constituents of the Department of Agriculture. University-oriented programs, he noted, are "good for forming partnerships, but not for growth opportunities."

Researchers at the Stanford Food Institute contend that

if existing technologies currently "on the shelf" were put to use, we could fill approximately half the international food gap by the year 2000, with a relatively small investment. A new breed of "super rice" developed by the International Rice Research Institute, for example, can potentially meet the needs of almost 450 million people.

The White House should take a hard look at ways to bolster the International Agricultural Research Centers (IARC), which we support through the Agency for International Development (AID). In theory, these centers pursue the high ground of research. But few have any real impact.

Blake recently visited a number of IARC sites, and asked administrators at each to name three vibrant research centers in the IARC network. "None were able to come up with three names," he said. The IARC could play a more significant role throughout the developing world if it were infused with meaningful support from donor countries.

Israel, as noted above, is a world leader in the agrotechnology field; her efforts should be substantially bolstered. Israel's Arava Valley is the only "growing" environment of its kind. With the Dead Sea to the north and the Red Sea to the south, the region's unique natural conditions, continual sunshine, and salubrious climate yield vegetables and fruits of unsurpassed quality that are in season throughout most of the year.

The Negev and Arava regions benefit from large amounts of underground warm and brackish water, a hydrological bounty for both intensive agriculture and intensive fish farming. The R&D Center for Pisciculture at Ein Yahav, located in the central Arav, has developed the technology to turn fish farming into a profitable commercial venture.

A model farm at Ein Yahav is based on the "chain of users" principle. Water released from fish ponds is channeled into the irrigation system for cultivating fruits and vegetables. Experiments in exploiting geothermic waters for fish farming are also being carried out at Moshav Kadesh Barnea.

Man and nature have joined forces in the ancient white sands of the Negev-Arava region to produce some of the finest products on earth. It would be an ironic pity and a global tragedy if these achievements were lost over time in a misguided mission by economists to dismantle Israel's agricultural sector.

For the moment, Jordan has conceded its territorial claims to the Arava. Jordanian and Israeli scientists, however, can be expected to join together in ongoing and new pilot projects. Agricultural advances in both countries, as well as in Egypt, Syria, and other Middle East countries, should be encouraged and shared with countries in Africa as well as with India, the Philippines, China, and Vietnam.

While irrigated lands account for 38 percent of world food, between 50 and 70 percent of the irrigation systems of the world need to be repaired, and most require modernization. A United States–led initiative in helping to replace both irrigation and urban water systems could make an impact at the most fundamental level. Replacement of Jordan's deteriorating municipal network, for instance, will cost about $135 million, and it will cost $6,500 per hectare to replace the country's irrigation system—donor agency monies well spent, if we consider the alternative.

Stemming Fundamentalism Through Food Security in Turkey

The 1994 water agreement between Turkey and Syria stated that Turkey will defend Syrian policy against Israel and the United States, and that Turkey will support Syrian policy on Lebanon. Ominously, this initiative was brokered by Iran, which is assiduously trying to cement relations with Turkey. In December 1993, Iran's Vice President Hassan Habibi and Foreign Minister Ali Akbar Velayati traveled to Ankara to help end the Turkish-Syrian dispute. In the darkest of scenarios, the Syrian-Iranian axis could be joined by Turkey, if the power of Turkey's radical fundamentalist factions spirals dangerously out of control.

Misguided U.S. policy may be at the root of these events. Syria's President Assad left his January 1994 Geneva meeting with Bill Clinton convinced that the U.S. president would back him on his demand for Israel to cede the entire Golan Heights, irrespective of Syria's ties with Iran. For Turkey, this meeting may have suggested that Syria would be a more valuable future ally than Israel.

The U.S. government had failed to help Turkey obtain long-sought admission to the European Economic Community, on which former prime minister and president Turgut Ozal had staked a large part of his political fortune. The White House also discouraged Turkey from cooperating with Russia in the former Soviet Muslim states, which left Turkey little choice but to increase its political cooperation with Iran in assisting these republics.

The diplomatic insecurity driving Turkey closer to Syria and Iran could be vastly reduced if Turkey's prospective role as food provider were properly recognized and rewarded. A food–self-sufficient country experiencing 7 percent annual growth, Turkey could be transformed into the breadbasket for large parts of the Middle East and Africa—if it received sufficient agricultural assistance from the United States.

Turkey currently meets the food demands of its population without recourse to importing major staples. But with a population increasing by 2.3 percent annually, and water as a constraining factor, the country is looking to increased yields as the only way to meet future demand.

Given present trends, Turkey will start importing wheat by the year 2000. However, through a sophisticated irrigation program, the education of farmers, better farming techniques, advanced farming technology, and the introduction of improved pesticide practices, Turkey's current croplands could be turned into a key part of the global solution instead of an additional part of the problem.

Until now, efforts by the Turkish government to elicit American government and private-sector assistance and participation has fallen on all-but deaf ears—putting the United States light years behind the French, Germans, and Japanese in responding to Turkey's agricultural potential. The president could immediately catapult the U.S. lag into a lead by mandating the secretary of commerce and the secretary of agriculture to make Turkey's agricultural sector a priority.

15

COVENANT OVER MIDDLE EASTERN WATERS

Water, thou hast no taste, no color, no odor; canst not be defined, art relished while ever mysterious. Not necessary to life, but rather life itself, thou fillest us with a gratification that exceeds the delight of the senses.

—Antoine de Saint-Exupéry,
Night Flight (1931)

Will Middle Easterners reach a lasting covenant over Middle East waters? Will they fulfill the spiritual water trust of their people?

An American network television interviewer recently asked this writer, "If Middle East leaders know that the region is facing imminent water dangers, why don't they just *do* something about it?"

My reply: If American leaders understand that nearly 50 million Americans are drinking water inadequately treated for toxic chemicals, bacteria, and human and animal waste, why haven't they *done* something about it? The principle is the same.

Nonetheless, Americans are culturally (and perhaps by

now genetically) programmed to believe there must be a solution for every problem. In this light, the solution to the Middle East water quagmire appears rather straightforward:

Water peace must somehow be achieved. To succeed, this process requires Syrian participation. Syria is not only a foe of Israel, but also one of the leading drug-smuggling nations on the planet, an ally of fundamentalist Iran, and a leading human rights violator. One would hope that if Syria makes water peace (or any peace) with Israel, it will cease all drug-smuggling activities, stop supporting Iranian terrorism, redirect its military budget to economic infrastructure, and welcome democracy at home.

Before rushing to the optimistic conclusion we all hope for, however, please note that the plot is slightly more complex. Counterfeiting, for example, from Iranian and Syrian operatives, is costing the United States billions of dollars each year.[1] Proceeds from these "superdollars" were likely channeled into terrorist activities such as the Iranian-linked car bombs that exploded in July 1994 next to the Israeli embassy in London, and in Jewish centers in both London and Argentina. These incidents were intended to coincide with the Jordanian-Israeli announcement that forty-eight years of "war" had officially ended.

Meanwhile, U.S. refineries continue to purchase up to 3.5 billion dollars of Iranian oil a year, Japan persists in financing Iranian dams, Russia maneuvers for profitable arms sales, and European businessmen keep the revolutionary state out of bankruptcy with commercial relations.

Secretary of State Warren Christopher, testifying before the House Foreign Affairs Committee on July 28, 1994, identified the Iranian-sponsored Hezbollah of Lebanon as being "at the bottom" of "perhaps all" the bombings, and U.S. diplomats have been trying to convince the Germans and Japanese to cease economic support for Teheran.

The Syrian government, moreover, has spent $1.4 billion on its military modernization programs since 1991, and is planning to begin production of its Scud-C tactical ballistic missile—which could negate Israeli air superiority—by mid-1996. The bulk of the $2.3 billion which Syria received as a reward from Saudi Arabia for joining the U.S.–led coalition against Iraq in the 1991 Gulf War has been spent on the military modernization program. Imagine if Syria were instead dedicating the funds, talents, and energies allocated to such feckless programs to regional water-management efforts.

Middle East water solutions—much less peace agreements—cannot be separated from drug smuggling, counterfeiting, fundamentalism, military/nuclear threats, and terrorism unless the true goal is to obscure reality with a pleasant prime-time picture.

"The value in dying at the hands of terrorists has greatly depreciated these days," wrote the *Jerusalem Post*'s Netty Gross in August 1994, as Israeli deaths from terrorist actions reached heights unseen since the Palestinian Intifada. "If going to Amman from Tel Aviv is going to be like going from New York to New Jersey, why are people still getting killed?" The solution to this riddle, she continued, "has been to democratize killing; such is the nature of Middle East crime."[2]

The Syrian and Israeli people deserve the opportunity to bridge the hostility separating them for almost half a century. But peace must be established over calm political waters.

Water Trust Based on Military Guarantees

The first frame to a happy ending to our tale would feature all parties to the Middle East conflict sitting at a grand oval table, perhaps with legs set in the Dead Sea; the leaders broadly smile at the cameras while they affix their signatures to a regional water-sharing treaty.

But at what price? The total dispute between Israel and Jordan, for example, was over the minuscule sum of 150 million cubic meters of water. After bickering for so many years, the parties finally settled at the annual compromise of 50 million cubic meters. Should this not be cause for celebration?

In reality, the 50 million cubic meters will buy Jordan a maximum of two years' additional water security, while the proposed upstream Yarmuk Dam could provide a further 100 million cubic meters of water respite. At the same time, as noted above, half of Jordan's water is lost through leaky pipes, and more than half of its Yarmuk River share has been diverted by Syria. "If Israel didn't exist," said the University of Jordan's Elias Salameh, "we still would have scarcity in the future. The cake is the same size; we can't enlarge it."[3]

If the Jordanians win the "battle" with Israel, but are left high and dry with Syria, and with insufficient international funds to tackle their most pressing infrastructure problems, theirs will be a hollow victory indeed.

Syria—which has an agreement with Jordan to draw 90 million cubic meters a year of Yarmuk waters—is simply "taking" 200 million, and there is absolutely nothing the Jordanians can do about it. Syrian attention to an equitable distribution of water, and to the repair of its antiquated, leaking water system, would greatly reduce overreliance on Yarmuk waters.

Syria still manages to provide 2,000 cubic meters of water for each of its citizens, while the Jordanian per capita share is only 280, and the Israeli share 380. Nevertheless, Israel is being asked by Washington, and by its Labor Party leadership, to relinquish eventually almost 30 percent of the country's water supply in return for "full peace." The Yarmuk River, flowing southward from the Golan Heights, supplies the Sea of Galilee with 610 million cubic meters annually.

Under the 1955 U.S.–sponsored Johnston plan, Israel was granted up to one-sixteenth of the Yarmuk flow, based on Israel's eight-mile shoreline along the river. Syrian attempts to divert these waters was a catalyst for the 1967 war. Israeli shelling of construction equipment across the Syrian frontier on March 17, 1967, was the warning shot over the bow.

Upon seizing the Golan Heights in 1967, Israel gained an extra twenty miles of river border, and access to 30 percent of the flow. Syria is calling for a return to the original division of waters. Israel further relies on Yarmuk waters to reduce salinity in the Sea of Galilee and to recharge its aquifers via its National Water Carrier.

Sovereignty over the Golan Heights is not, as many believe, a black-and-white issue. The Bashan Region (the Biblical name of the Golan Heights, as promised to Patriarch Abraham) was settled by half the tribe of Manasseh during the First Temple period. Babylonian exiles lived among the people of the region during the period of the Second Temple, and Jewish settlements placed their roots there for seven hundred years after it was conquered by King Alexander Yanai at the end of the Hasmonaean period.

Archaeological discoveries in the Golan include twenty-five synagogues from the Talmudic period. Jewish groups purchased land and lived on the Golan through the 1947 War of Independence, when the land was seized by Syria. Israel gained formal control over the Golan Heights on June 10, 1967, the last day of the Six Day War.

Even if Syria and Israel forge a peace agreement in 1995 or 1996, water contentions over the Golan Heights could continue for years to come. An Israeli government that concedes territory on the Golan without a guaranteed supply of Yarmuk waters, or a dedicated alternative source of water, would be committing national suicide. It could take almost a decade, not to mention billions of dollars of investment, to create an alternative water supply sufficient for Israel, the West Bank, and Gaza. Moreover, each of the proposed "solutions" bandied about in Middle East forums carries its own baggage of weaknesses and dangers.

Why, then, would Israel voluntarily relinquish vital waters, when Syria has so little political leverage? And why would the United States serve as the impassioned matchmaker for a hasty Israeli-Syrian embrace?

Addressing the Syrian parliament on September 10, 1994, President Assad stated that "Syria realizes the importance of a peace that ensures full Israeli withdrawal from the Golan Heights . . . and will meet the objective requirements agreed upon."

Prime Minister Rabin asserted that Assad's words conveyed acceptance of the "objective conditions of peace," yet also admitted that the Syrian's words in fact represented only a "slight change" in Syria's public diplomacy. But an Israeli foreign ministry official was more revealing in explaining the forces prodding both Rabin and Assad—with the courting services of American officials—to a behind-the-scenes quick step:

"We don't have more than a few months" to reach agreement with Syria, he disclosed, because otherwise elections in both the United States and Israel could put the peace process on hold. "If we are not signing an agreement in the coming months, it might wait for the beginning of 1997."[4]

The Syrians, to their diplomatic "credit," have not tried to obfuscate or otherwise hide their water intentions. To the contrary, Syrian leaders made it publicly clear as recently as the beginning of 1994 that Syria cannot spare "one drop" of water for Israel. "The Golan is Syrian territory," stated Nasir Qaddur, Syrian minister of state for foreign affairs, at a January 13, 1994, press conference. "Syria needs water. . . . The water reserves are not enough to meet Syria's requirements."

Qaddur continued: "We have irrigation and electricity projects in the east of the country, and any shortfall in the water will result in the depopulation of the area. Syria does not have enough water to spare for Israel."

Anything short of an ironclad agreement on Golan military and water security would be a reckless policy choice for Israel. The key question: Is the United States in a position to guarantee that peace is worth the water price through the placement of troops on the Golan? The most active terrorists in the world, it should be recalled, are operating out of Syria and Lebanon.

Our hearts and military are in the right place. Politically, however, the last superpower is losing its will for confrontation. According to one recent poll, 75 percent of Americans supported humanitarian intervention during the 1992 Somalian episode; by the time U.S. troops reached the Rwanda-Zaire border in July 1994, only half the people polled thought the United States had a duty to intervene abroad in either disasters or potentially explosive conflict situations.

Based on the American foreign policy track record in Somalia, Rwanda, and Bosnia, the longevity of future U.S. political commitments under fire—or as in the case of Lebanon, in the face of shifting political alignments—should give one reason to ponder. According to an exhaustive study by Dore Gold, a researcher with Israel's left-of-center Jaffee Center for Strategic Studies, "the Golan could be a far greater risk for American forces, if a future regime resorted to terrorism to harass the force and bring the American presence to a premature end." Gold concluded that "turning to the U.S. as a source of security on the Golan . . . would not be in Israel's long-term interest."[5]

The prospect of an Israeli/Syrian agreement being backed up by United Nations troops and bureaucracy is even more questionable. With due respect to the UN's merits, this is the very same organization that launched a private war in Somalia leading to the death of U.S. soldiers; that couldn't provide sufficient trucks to get U.S. food supplies to starving Rwandans; and whose peace-keeping efforts in Bosnia turned into a moral and operational disaster. It was also a UN committee that released a report in mid-1994 accusing Israel of stealing Lebanon's water. Similar charges were repudiated years ago not only by U.S. government intelligence experts, but also by senior Lebanese officials.

The region's water future requires extraordinary leadership and vision, not the salvo offer of American or United Nations troops.

Syria's fears and requirements must be equitably addressed. Nevertheless, before we attempt to "liberate" the Golan Heights from Israel, we should first consider liberating water-blessed Lebanon from Syrian domination. To fortify Lebanon as a sovereign state, and as a democratic bridge between Syria and Israel, could prove a dramatic confidence-building measure. To bring Lebanon to the table as an active member in the regional water dialogue could also prove the first concrete step toward a solution.

Water Security Framework

An enduring Middle East water security framework demands: parallel planning and policy coordination between countries; mediation and conciliation; regional data collection; project identification; sufficient financing for the repair and construction of infrastructure; and an infusion of monies into research and development in related fields.

Three years of discussions under the umbrella of the Middle East Multilateral Water Commission have produced the first steps toward regional data collection; several small but worthy sewage and pipe-repair pilot projects; and a new center for desalination research in Qatar, with Israeli scientists invited to participate in the research process.

The technical experts within Middle East governments understand that the status quo is a life-limiting sentence, not a blessing. These experts have reached broad agreement that water supplies should be increased; that major water transfers from one country to another are not a realistic option; and that the most practical approach to water security is vastly improved water management.

That it took almost three years to reach these riveting conclusions (which echo myriads of UN and international conference statements), or that Syria, and consequently Lebanon, refused to participate in any of the deliberations, does not negate the value of the process. Nevertheless, the vision and political leadership required to pull the region from the quicksand of its disappearing water future is yet to be demonstrated. The current goal, it appears, is centered more on finger-in-the-dike measures than on a revolution of enduring water peace.

The globally televised signing of the peace agreement between Jordan and Israel, an exhilarating moment for mankind, also led to great hyperbole about the transformation of the "brown desert" of the Arava into a green paradise. But anyone who has been privileged to absorb the solemn beauty of the Arava would find it difficult to fathom either the portrait or the prospect.

To the contrary, a heedless dash down the path of overdevelopment could turn the pristine grace of this special desert into a brown, sullen landscape, while draining the waters of survival from the region's remaining green terrain.

Only the World's Elite Get Their Water from the Sea

There is little long-term water hope for Jordan, or for West Bank and Gaza Palestinians, without the state of Israel.

Palestinian negotiators demand that the mountain aquifer be ceded to their autonomous authority, and argue that Israel can simply live off of desalinated seawater. "We don't need to produce more water," said a Palestinian negotiator to an Israeli colleague. "You are the one with the problem."

Some water experts claim that for $3.5 billion, sufficient desalination plants could be built to satisfy the future needs of all parties to the Holy Land water conflict.

Others reply: Had God been asked to provide an environmental impact statement, he would have said, "If you so insist, I shall not create the world." It could take five years to obtain approvals for a scheme of desalination plants, and as many as twenty years from the feasibility study to the final construction.

Until now, Israel has resisted substantial investment in desalination, as there was no measurable need. The country still has an annual water supply of approximately 1.6 billion cubic meters, with only 600 million being used for urban purposes.

Desalted seawater costs one thousand to two thousand dollars per acre-foot, as compared to the three hundred dollars per acre-foot that the world's average urban dweller pays for delivered water. Farmers, relying on government subsidies, pay much less.

"Whenever I say there is a shortage of water, the economists always say that they can prove it is not so," said Uri Marinov, former director general of Israel's Ministry of the Environment. "True, the technology is here. But at what cost? I cannot see how desalinated water can be used for agriculture."[6]

Technologically speaking, Israel can solve its drinking water problem by gradually developing desalination plants along the coast in response to increasing demand. Since the interface between seawater and groundwater is not along the seashore, but 1.5 kilometers inland, the underground aquifer would not be endangered. This approach, however, will require a high degree of confidence that imported energy will be continuously available or, alternatively, that the price of solar energy for desalination can be greatly reduced (not likely in the foreseeable future). Desalination means dependency on energy.

In the Mediterranean, to choose desalination is a de facto decision to accept reliance on imported energy. Yet, given the potency of Islamic fundamentalism throughout the Middle East, assumptions about a constant supply of energy could be hazardous to a nation's health.

Desalination along the seashore has the advantage of placing production and demand in the same spot. But consumption is never linear. We do not consume at night as we do during the day, although machines must continue to function. If the Israeli coastal aquifer is covered by concrete, where will the water be stored?

Desalination's high energy use runs counter to the goals of reducing air pollution, acid rain, greenhouse gas emissions, and fossil fuel dependence. And according to officials with the U.S. National Oceanic and Atmospheric Administration (NOAA), the cumulative effects of drawing water from and discharging brine into the ocean have not been studied.

A recent World Watch investigation concluded that boiling water or pushing it through membranes requires substantial energy—roughly 6,000 kilowatt-hours per acre-foot for the most effective methods. To desalt 100 percent of residential waters anywhere would raise electricity use by one-third. Solar desalination would eliminate high energy bills, but low output and high equipment costs would still make it more expensive.

Desalination's high costs are compounded by corrosion and clogging of equipment—including algae and other organic matter that foul salt-filtering membranes—and the disposal of pretreatment sludges and postprocess brines. This would explain why most of the world's desalting capacity is found in water-poor, but rich states like Saudi

Arabia, Kuwait, and the United Arab Emirates. "It will never be cheap water," said a NOAA scientist.

Peace or Pie Canals?

"Every minister with his own canal!" chides former Israeli water commissioner Dan Zaslavsky. "Our agriculture minister wants a desalination canal, our energy minister an energy canal, the foreign minister a political canal. Each one made different promises to the Arabs. My worst fear is that someone will actually commit us to a pie-in-the-sky plan."

While the newspapers gobble up dramatic announcements of a seawater peace canal between Israel and Jordan, the potential mistakes could be historic in dimension. "We're not talking about small mistakes in economic calculations," said Zaslavsky. "These plans are typically miscalculated by a magnitude of minus 400 to 500 percent.

"I cannot think of a more stupid thing to do," he added, before all available "niches," such as desalting brackish water, have been explored. "The ministers simply do not understand," he said. "It is not even important to them to listen. They do not see themselves as consumers of expertise." The person responsible for "planning" in the office of the water commissioner, he noted wryly, has a degree in social work—and is sweetly protected in this sinecure by Israel's civil service.

"It is clear that Israelis, Palestinians, and Jordanians require additional sources of water from a nonnatural source," declared Meir Ben-Meir. "But where and how is a question for careful study." Senior echelons in Israel and Jordan recognize that additional water for urban purposes must be introduced by the beginning of the coming century if a crisis is to be averted.

The primary schemes under consideration involve seawater desalination—either through the construction of desalination plants along the shore of the Mediterranean or, alternatively, along the Syrian-African depression between the Lake of Galilee and the Dead Sea.[7]

The seashore alternative is technologically simple and would substitute for pumping from the coastal aquifer. Construction can also be staged according to a gradual increase in demand, since plants would be located only a short distance from urban centers.

The morc complicated alternatives involve the creation of pipe-systems to transport hundreds of million cubic meters of seawater to a chosen location along the Syrian-African depression. While the seashore approach is characterized by low capital investment and high energy costs, the latter would involve high capital investment, but low energy costs. Electricity would be generated by the fall of water from the sea level of the Mediterranean to the depths of the Dead Sea, the lowest spot on earth.

Water obtained by desalination along the Syrian-African depression, however, is constrained by the annual evaporation of the Dead Sea, since the sea would serve as the receptacle for the brine derived from the proposed desalting plants. In the seashore alternative, by contrast, thc brine would be disposed directly into the Mediterranean, and the potential quantities of water produced would be unlimited.

A Jordanian presentation to the Multilateral Water Committee in September 1992 noted that conveyance, capital, and running costs of a Red Sea–Dead Sea (Red-Dead) canal would be prohibitive. Only two years later, however,

Israeli and Jordanian ministers were touting the proposed canal as a priority for joint Israeli-Jordanian development of drinking water—suggesting that it could help bring to pass the prophetic vision of the Hebrew Prophet Ezekiel that fish would one day thrive in the Dead Sea.

Unfortunately, at a cost of at least $2.50 per cubic meter, Palestinians could not survive on desalinated waters garnered from such a canal for their drinking water needs.

A proposed Mediterranean–Dead Sea (Med-Dead) canal shares all the disadvantages of a Red-Dead canal, and would also cut through the earthquake-prone landscape of the African-Syrian break or fault line. "The Med-Dead should remain a dead corpse," said a senior Israeli environmental official. "It is not economically feasible and will ruin part of the Jordan valley."

Mining, Sewage, Clouds, and Floodwater

Sewage is an endless resource. Sixty-five percent of every cubic meter of domestic water consumed can be salvaged and channeled to agriculture, as long as the cost is lower than that of the alternative source (desalination).

Israel's freshwater for urban purposes is treated by Mekorot, the national water company. Human, industrial, and agricultural pollution, unfortunately, flows primarily to the seashore aquifer.

Theory suggests that both urban and agricultural sectors are helping each other if their approach to sewage reclamation is cooperative. The urban sector has an obligation to purify sewage for environmental and human reasons, and the agricultural sector has an interest in absorbing treated sewage after giving it additional treatment. The urban sector also wants to rid itself of pollution created by treated sewage. The agricultural sector, left without a drop of freshwater, will demand, absorb, and rely upon treated sewage.

The more artificial water produced, the more treated sewage can be allocated for agricultural purposes. The only question is whether the Israeli government, as well as other Middle East nations, will be skilled enough to ensure that the cost to the farmers for reclaimed and transported sewage will not reach the expense level of desalinated water.

Once the cost of treatment and recycling reaches the cost of desalination, agriculture in Israel is doomed. Farmers will not be able to cover such high prices through returns on their crops. The country and its municipalities must be efficient enough to provide treated sewage at a low price.

Now for the argument between the farmers of Israel and the water company, Mekorot: The farmers insist that Mekorot should be responsible for drinking water, while they should be responsible for treated sewage so they can farm the land at a reasonable price. "If the government will not be sensitive enough to overcome the monopolistic resistance of Mekorot, then the young yuppies of the treasury will be correct when they say that it makes no sense to continue farming the land of Israel. For at that point, it will simply be too expensive," said Ben-Meir.

The farmers believe they could operate the treatment system at roughly 20 percent of what Mekorot charges the government. Until now, however, their municipalities have not been strong enough to take the profits away from Mekorot.

As of late 1994, work had not yet begun on a sewage

master plan for Israel. The government did, however, approve a general line of inquiry: Where should the sewage of urban areas be utilized; to what standards; for what purposes; and should the reclaimed sewage be used above aquifers, or only where there is no aquifer below?

Wastewater could also provide a key portion of renewable resource for Jordan, but at a high cost in treatment technology and environmental safeguards.

Nearly 45 percent of Jordan's population is connected to a sewage system. However, most villages rely on cesspits to collect wastewater, and these discharges eventually reach the groundwater system. Jordanian attempts to use brackish water for irrigation are both promising and dangerous, as they lead to higher soil salinity and contamination of groundwater supplies beneath the irrigated areas.

Based on these factors, the Jordanian government has concluded that while wastewater treatment and reuse can play a significant role in diverting freshwater from agriculture to municipal use, wastewater, on its own, cannot ensure the expansion of agricultural production. Treated effluent will barely be sufficient to grow 5 percent of Jordan's required agricultural production.[8]

Jordan has also dismissed the importation of water as the solution to its water dilemma. A joint study (1981–1984) conducted with Iraq on the diversion of the Euphrates from Iraq to Amman noted that high capital and operating costs would mean a cost of two dollars per cubic meter for water delivery to Amman, while the safety and security of sustained supplies could not be ensured.

Israel has made major advances in cloud-seeding technology; the literature suggests that as much as a 10-percent increase in rainfall can be achieved in some areas. Jordan, however, believes that "while cloud seeding may be a modest source to enhance water supply, much of its characteristics is yet to be investigated. Its positive and negative environmental impacts should also be assessed and its economic feasibility be better understood."[9]

More than 1 million cubic meters of floodwater flowing from the Jordan into the Dead Sea are also wasted. Manmade reservoirs, however, can capture winter floodwater and hold it for summer use. The Jewish National Fund has established over forty such reservoirs in Israel.

The Cost of Water

Adam Smith pointed out the paradox in the fact that freshwater, which is vital for the sustenance of all life, costs nothing, whereas diamonds, which are vital for nothing at all, cost so much.

The Mideast region has the highest median cost of water supply and sanitation in the world; capital costs reached a median of three hundred dollars per capita in 1985, about twice those in the United States and more than five times the costs in Southeast Asia.

Israel, Jordan, and Tunisia are the only Middle East countries that have tariff systems for municipal and industrial water use; Israel is the sole country that also charges a reasonable tariff for irrigation water. The minimal fees levied by other regional nations hardly recover even the costs of system operation and maintenance. Water bills in Saudi Arabia are one-tenth of those in Western nations.

But even in Israel, where water does have a price, municipalities use large parts of the money collected as water fees for purposes other than water and sewage. There have been attempts to pass a law prohibiting this practice, but the Ministry of the Treasury and the Ministry of the Interior have so far blocked it.

A key achievement would be agreement between Israelis and Palestinians on the cost of water, with the channeling of proceeds to water and sewage infrastructure. Charges must be based on the real expense of providing water, and a closed accounting system must be created so that all monies charged by municipalities are used exclusively for water and not to generate revenues for other purposes.

Efficient pricing must be combined with proper internal management and, no less importantly, with effective cooperation between countries. Why, for example, should the Persian Gulf states be using their finite oil and gas energy to distill water for growing wheat when Lebanon's waters are flowing into the ocean? Gulf nations could be rechanneling oil funds to pay poorer countries for available water, while saving their energy, and our global inheritance, for world prosperity.

Treatment and distribution of water are expensive. Thousands of dollars per capita are tied up in any public utility or water company, for pipes, pumping stations, treatment plants, dams, and the like.

Privatization of public water and sewage companies, with its potential for assuring the most effective use of physical, human, and financial resources, should be considered. This can take the form of management leasing, where assets are still owned by the government public utility, but operated through a private management contract. England's water systems are fully privatized, while France claims a mixture of privatization schemes. Beyond these two countries, however, the idea of privatization of water systems, let alone of sewage systems, is just beginning to take hold.

A Rooted Approach

Most inhabitants of the Middle East still believe that, since water comes from God, it is their natural birthright to exploit it as they wish. The fact that water has an economic value, and that its availability is diminished by accelerating population growth, must be communicated, beginning at the grade school level. Middle Eastern leaders, as well as their Western partners, must accelerate efforts to explain to the grassroots public the effects of spiraling population on finite water resources.

A key is the education and empowerment of women. The September 1994 UN Population Conference at Cairo reached firm consensus that the single variable with the greatest impact on population size is female literacy. The resulting Cairo document gave primacy to the needs of women in family planning, and in educational, economic, and political opportunities.

Saudi Arabia and the Sudan unfortunately boycotted the conference, while Iran tried to thwart a final resolution.[10] The moral power of this event notwithstanding, the resolutions are nonbinding on world governments.

A multidisciplinary and "rooted" approach to water is imperative as we enter a new era in the struggle for water supply. The foundation of this approach must include wide-scale education of the public on the meaning and value of water; coordinated planning of water and agricultural sectors among all basin countries; sewage reclamation as a first priority; aquifer cleanup; pollution control; correct pricing of water; and most significantly, respect for the land.

If, on the other hand, Middle Eastern leaders persist in reaching for spectacularly expensive technological solutions over less glamorous but essential steps, current resources will vanish in the flash of twenty-five years, with no redress.

Rescue by massive desalination or billion-dollar white-elephant canals will by then be remembered only as pipe dreams from the past.

The Whole of My Wealth

The tale of the fifteenth-century monarch of Sri Lanka, King Dhatusena, is illustrative of a time when water was venerated. When the king was taken prisoner by a rebel army led by his son, Prince Kahsyapa, his captors demanded of Dhatusena that he show where the royal treasure was hidden. The king led them to Kalaweva, an artificial lake with a circumference of ninety kilometers, which had been constructed during his reign. At the lakeshore he took a handful of water and showed it to them, saying: "This, my friends, is the whole of my wealth."

"The world, too, has something like a soul," said Czechoslovak President Václav Havel. This is more than a "mere body of information that can be externally grasped and objectified and mechanically assembled." Man should not be just an observer or a manager of the world, he cautioned, but part of the world.[11]

A politician, Havel said, must trust not only an objective interpretation of reality, not only an adopted ideology, but also his own thoughts—not only the summary reports he receives each morning, but also his own feelings. The arrogant belief that the world is a puzzle to be objectively analyzed and solved must be abandoned.

Statistics, engineering plans, and new technologies—if

properly evaluated—can make a vital contribution. As we have seen, however, it is the leaders and decision-makers, the water caretakers, who bear ultimate responsibility for tomorrow's water scarcity, pollution, and drought.

"Dashed hopes," said Vice President Al Gore in a 1994 Harvard commencement address, "poison our political will just as surely as chemical waste can poison drinking water aquifers deep in the ground. . . . The results are for all to see."

If we are fortunate, the powerful will recognize, in time, that the true path to Middle East water peace, and to the world's water survival, must begin from the heart.

CONCLUSION

The Prologue Is Our Future

I have come to believe that all of the earth's rivers, seas, streams, and underground waters emanate from the waters of creation.

In Judaic, Muslim, and Christian traditions, the source of the waters of life is believed to lie beneath the very piece of earth that rests at the heart of a final Middle East peace settlement: Jerusalem.

Our spiritual forefathers taught that the waters of creation flowed from the Temple Mount of Jerusalem. The sacred texts upon which much of modern Middle Eastern thinking is based recognized Jerusalem's special energy. Thus, political contention over the City of Gold, the holiest site on the planet, may be viewed not merely as a dispute over land, but as a cosmic battle over the sacred waters of life.

Mideast leaders are painting the future of the region with pigments that are water-based. Unfortunately, most seem generally unmoved by the cosmic sanctity of water, much less by its deeply rooted effect on the emotions and convictions of their people.

Yet failure to revere these sweet waters, the mystical land from which they flow, and their life-sustaining vegetation could eventually leave only tears of bitterness to quench our thirst, and parched lands to feed our hunger.

✦ ✦ ✦

I stopped by to see Lot's Wife in June 1994, less than a year after our first meeting. A team of archaeologists was engaged in animated debate in a nearby cave over the future of the salt mountain on which she stood. As I entered the cave, carved over millions of years by the salty waters of the Dead Sea, I felt an integral part of that passage of time.

Intending to hurry, I lingered instead, mentally replaying my earlier search for release from troubled Middle Eastern waters. Hoping for a sign—a rock that would fall, a whisper that would lead me to understanding—I had felt, at the time, that Lot's Wife had somehow disappointed me. But as I again looked up at this monument, I realized that the very act of traveling back to the past to meet her had been the dawn of my understanding. A tranquil feeling supplanted my foreboding from the previous year's visit.

I had come to appreciate the meaning of Lot's Wife, her salty presence, her purpose.

Lot's Wife was a signpost, a memorial, programmed by God as an alarm to awaken us thousands of years later. Cast as our silent siren, she was turned into salt to remind us of the lessons of Sodom and Gomorrah: Learn to care for one another, and to share, where possible.

When a people's security is threatened by sharing, we must seek creative solutions to help to ensure that none will suffer from thirst. But this search can succeed only if the requirements of the present, as well as the needs of the future, are wedded with the insights of our forefathers.

The waters of the Dead Sea, guarded by Lot's Wife, may

indeed carry the secret code, the key, to the survival of the planet: Ignore the lesson of Lot's Wife, and our life-giving freshwaters could turn into seas of death.

The woman who looked only backward suffered a sad and lonely ending. We, on the other hand, must look forward together, in balance and in harmony with nature and her creatures.

Lot's Wife guided this traveler toward the wisdom of the sages, and the echo was heard: Pay homage to our ancient waters as you would to a beloved parent or esteemed teacher. Treat them as your most honored and cherished guest.

NOTES

1. Deities and Powers

1. Gerald L. Schroeder, *Genesis and the Big Bang: The Discovery of Harmony Between Modern Science and the Bible* (New York: Bantam, 1990), pp. 120–121.
2. Nostradamus's writings are decoded in V. J. Hewitt and Peter Lorie, *Nostradamus: The End of the Millennium* (New York: Simon & Schuster, 1991).
3. Paul J. Achtemeier, ed., *Harper's Bible Dictionary* (San Francisco: Harper & Row, 1985), p. 232.
4. N. K. Sanders, *The Epic of Gilgamesh* (London: Penguin Books, 1972), p. 108. This epic is also the first recorded source of Turkish folklore. Scholars have determined that a king named Gilgamesh indeed lived and reigned in Uruk during the first half of the third millennium.
5. Ibid., p. 108.
6. Ibid., p. 112.

2. Divine Waters

1. Rabbi Shlomo Riskin, "The Land: A Gift from the Creator," *Jerusalem Post*, international ed., May 1994, p. 23.
2. *Interpreter's Dictionary of the Bible* (Nashville: Abingdon-Cokesbury Press, 1962), p. 705.
3. For a further discussion of the *mikvah* and the significance of "liv-

ing waters,'' please see Dr. Philip S. Berg, *Kabbalah for the Layman* (Jerusalem: Press of the Research Center of the Kabbalah, 1981), p. 40, 180.

4. Terence Kleven, ''Up the Water Spout: How David's General Joab Got Inside Jerusalem,'' *Biblical Archaeology Review*, July–August 1994, page 34.
5. Israel Finkelstein and David Ussiskin, ''Back to Megiddo,'' *Biblical Archaeology Review*, January–February 1994, p. 28.
6. Dan Cole, ''How Water Tunnels Work,'' *Biblical Archaeology Review*, March–April 1980, pp. 8–29.
7. Ibid.
8. Background on the Nile, Khosr, and Babylonian water diversions appear in Haeh Hatami and Peter H. Gleick, ''Conflicts over Water in the Myths, Legends, and Ancient History of the Middle East,'' *Environment*, April 1994, pp. 10–11.

3. *Ishmael and the Well of Water*

1. John Sabini, *Islam: A Primer* (Washington, D.C.: Middle East Editorial Associates, 1990), pp. 63, 119.
2. Ibid., p. 67.
3. This section is based upon C. E. Bosworth, E. van Donzel, B. Lewis, and Ch. Pellat, eds., *The Encyclopedia of Islam* (Leiden: E. J. Brill, 1983), pp. 859–889.
4. Alan Cowell, *New York Times*, May 9, 1989, p. A6.

4. *Water Poker: Playing for Our Lives*

1. Author's interview, March 1992.
2. Priit Vasiland, ''Middle East Water,'' *National Geographic*, May 1993, p. 67.
3. Ibid.
4. ''Use of Force to Protect Nile Not Ruled Out,'' *Egyptian Gazette*, October 10, 1991, p. 2.
5. Sandra Postel, *The Last Oasis* (New York: W. W. Norton, 1992), p. 31.
6. Vasiland, p. 68.
7. Author's interview, August 1991.

5. Searching for the Holy Grain

1. *Middle East,* July 1985, p. 14.
2. Based on International Food Policy Research Institute, *Food in the Third World: Past Trends and Projections to 2000,* Research Report 52 (June 1986), p. 43, and on subsequent report assessments.
3. *Christian Science Monitor,* December 18, 1987.
4. Peter Beaumont, *Trends in Middle East Agriculture,* ed. by P. Beaumont and K. McLachlan (New York: John Wiley, 1985), p. 321.
5. Lester Brown, remarks before the World Economic Forum, Davos, Switzerland, January 1992.
6. Per Pinstrup-Andersen, 1992 Environmental and Energy Study Institute briefing on Capitol Hill.

6. The Desert May Not Bloom Here Anymore: Israel

1. Author's interview, Tel Aviv, May 1994.
2. Author's interview, Tel Aviv, July 1993.
3. Liat Collins, "Threatened by Peace," *Jerusalem Post,* international ed., Aug 20, 1994, p. 16B.
4. Ibid.
5. Author's interview.
6. Author's interview, Lod area, September 1993.

8. Armageddon Underground?

1. "Nation's Drinking Water Below Western Standards," *Jerusalem Post,* May 19, 1994.
2. Author's interview.
3. Evelyn Gordon, "Industrial Pollution from Autonomous Areas Could Threaten Water Supply," *Jerusalem Post,* June 1, 1994, p. 14.
4. "Nation's Drinking Water."
5. Author's interview.
6. See the State Comptroller's Report, 1994.
7. Itamar Marcus, "The Hand That Controls the Faucet Rules the Country," *Jerusalem Post,* July 10, 1994, p. 7.

8. Ibid.
9. Ibid.
10. Ibid.
11. Ibid.
12. Ibid.

9. The Gate of No Return: From Israel to Jordan

1. Background on the history of the Jordan Valley is drawn from Rami G. Khouri, *The Jordan Valley* (Harlow, Essex: Longman Group, 1981), pp. 1–42.
2. Ibid., p. 28.
3. Author's interview, Washington, D.C., October 25, 1994.
4. The author is grateful to Uri Baidats, chairman of Israel's Nature Reserves Authority, for his introduction to the wonders of the Dan and Banias nature reserves.

10. The Water Summit That Wasn't

Chapter epigraph from author's interview, August 1991.

12. Syria's Peril, Lebanon's Plenty

1. The author wishes to acknowledge the research efforts of Susan Medlin, Captain, US Army, and her paper, "Syria's Water Problems," submitted to the Faculty of the Joint Military Intelligence College, June 28, 1994.

13. Saddam's Atrocious Little War Against the Garden of Eden

1. Caryle Murphy, "Iraq Withering Under Economic and Political Isolation, State Repression," *Washington Post,* July 24, p. A23.
2. "Hopeful Foreign Businessmen Flocking to Iraq," *Washington Post,* July 13, 1994.

14. Caretakers and Redeemers

1. *Washington Post,* June 24, 1994, p. A3.
2. "Is Your Water Safe: The Dangerous State of Drinking Water in America," special report, *U.S. News & World Report,* July 29, 1991.
3. *Washington Post,* October 18, 1994.
4. Molly Moore, "Around Globe, Water Quality Is Matter of Life and Death," *Washington Post,* Dec. 12, 1993, p. A39.
5. Ibid.
6. Ibid.
7. *Washington Post,* "Outlook" section, February 27, 1994.
8. Steve LeVine, "Aral Sea's Defenders Suspend Fight to Save It," *Washington Post,* September 9, 1994, p. A3.
9. Korinna Horta, "Monster of the Himalayas: The World Bank's Misconceived Mega-Project in the Heart of Nepal," *Washington Post,* November 6, 1994, p. C4.
10. Discussion with author, New York, March 1992.
11. Author's interview, June 1993.

15. Covenant over Middle Eastern Waters

1. Jack Anderson and Michael Binstein, "Hitting Back at 'Super Greenbacks,' " *Washington Post,* July 28, 1994, p. D19.
2. "Terror Victims' Families Now Grieve Alone," *Jerusalem Post,* international ed., August 20, 1994, p. 6.
3. Priit Vasiland, "Middle East Water," *National Geographic,* May 1993, p. 59.
4. Caryle Murphy, "Israel, Syria Display a Growing Flexibility," *Washington Post,* September 13, 1994, p. A12.
5. Dore Gold, "US Forces on the Golan Heights and Israeli-Syrian Security Arrangements," Jaffee Center for Strategic Studies, Tel Aviv University, memorandum no. 44 (August 1994), p. 49.
6. Author's interview, May 1994.
7. The author wishes to acknowledge the efforts of engineer Shlomo Gur, who has devoted the remaining years of his life to a proposal for a Jezreel canal carrier, linking the Mediterranean with the Jordan River through the Jezreel and Beth-Shean valleys. By dint of his persistence, Gur has succeeded in creating spirited debate over the different canal options.

8. Jordanian government presentation before the Multilateral Working Group on Water, October 1992, p. 13.
9. Ibid.
10. *Washington Post,* Friday, August 12, 1994.
11. Speaking before the World Economic Forum, Davos, Switzerland, January 1992.

INDEX